TRANSCENDING ANXIETY

FROM FEAR TO

Freedom

Manal El-Ramly

Cover design by: Matt Davies

Editing by: Sage Taylor Kingsley SageforYourPage.com

Hardcover: # 979-8-9893859-2-8
Paperback: # 979-8-9893859-1-1
Electronic: # 979-8-9893859-0-4

Revised Edition

Published by Mattain Publishing, LLC

www.mattain.com

DISCLAIMER

The intent of the author is to provide personal life lessons and information of a general nature to assist you with self-discovery and the pursuit of holistic well-being. You agree that if you use the information or suggestions provided in this book, the author and publisher cannot be held liable or responsible for any loss, claim, or damage allegedly arising from your actions. If you have any health concerns, please be sure to consult with a medical professional. This book aims to offer insights and tools for better understanding your full being, whatever your current physical or health situation may be. Please note that this resource is not intended as a substitute for professional medical advice, diagnosis, or treatment from qualified healthcare professionals. Some names have been changed to protect privacy; however, all case studies reflect true success stories using The Mattain Method.

Mom and Dad:

Without you,

I would not be *here*.

I love you,

Manal

Contents

LIST OF FIGURES

"It's hard, until it's not."

AN INTRODUCTION

Truth: Know it. Trust it. Feel it. Be it.

I've always needed to understand *why*. Why am I here? Why is life the way it is? This need to understand myself and the world around me has been with me my whole life. From an early age, I questioned everything: What is the meaning of life? How come our lives are all so different, yet the same?

The values my parents—who immigrated from Egypt to Canada seeking freedom—instilled in me have shaped my ambition of finding answers to life's big questions. They hold strong convictions regarding religion, charity, and leading a virtuous life. My dad, an academic and entrepreneur, fostered my love for logic and intellectual pursuits. My mom, with her boundless empathy and commitment to family, shaped my values of compassion and love. Their dedication to family, education, entrepreneurship, and the delicate balance between drive and acceptance of life has inspired me to continually seek wisdom, growth, service, and surrender.

Before diving in, let's clarify one thing. Though I've had the privilege of coaching thousands of people in a myriad of settings, I'm not a doctor, therapist, or counselor. I see myself as a *student of life*. While the results others have achieved by working with me have certainly motivated, validated, and fine-tuned my methodology, most of my wisdom comes from personal experiences, interpersonal connections, and an insatiable passion for uncovering truth.

The central premise of this book is rooted in a foundational truth: anxiety, at its core, is unacknowledged fear.

This guiding perspective, and the framework presented in these pages, emerged from a rich mosaic of experiences—my life experiences, the lessons of motherhood (often life's greatest teacher), professional work with clients, bonds with family and friends, societal observations, and inquisitive reflections on life. By examining the root causes of unacknowledged fears, particularly three primary ones I'll soon uncover, we can address and alleviate anxiety more effectively.

This book will guide you through the integral layers of your being—Physical, Emotional, Mental, and Egoic—or what I term the "The Four Bodies."

The Four Bodies represent the different facets of yourself that contribute to your overall experience of life.

The Physical Body is your tangible presence in the world, encompassing your physical sensations, well-being, and unique embodied physical self.

The Emotional Body is the landscape of your emotions, where you feel a wide range of states from joy and love to sadness and anger.

The Mental Body is the domain of your thoughts, logic, and perceptions, where you process information and make sense of yourself and the world around you.

The Egoic Body is the center of your identity and "seat of your soul" (a term deeply illuminated by Gary Zukav), where you define your sense of self, values, core beliefs, and connection to greater meaning and purpose.

Tuning into the wisdom of The Four Bodies is crucial. Each serves a unique purpose. While society praises our mental and physical capabilities, it generally neglects our emotional and egoic expressions. In these pages, I'll guide you through The Four Bodies, lighting the path for you to embrace and live from your complete self. This expanded awareness will ignite greater harmony, wholeness, and freedom, leading to the realization of your truest "I AM."

You might be wondering what prompted me to unpack the subject of anxiety and bring this book to life. I wonder at times, too! My path to becoming a life coach and the founder of Mattain LLC— a self-growth coaching and media company dedicated to helping others evolve beyond life's struggles and discover their inner truth—has been diverse and enriching.

My academic background, including bachelor's and master's degrees in mechanical engineering, infused me with a rigorous foundation for analytical thinking. My career and personal experiences have spanned fields as broad as consulting, technology, entrepreneurship, education, functional medicine, spirituality, and the most rewarding of them all: parenting. Although my initial forays into these areas were not aimed at unraveling the complexities of human experience, the cumulative wisdom I've gained eventually coalesced into a holistic understanding of human behavior.

In addition to a wide range of personal and professional experiences, I've always been an avid reader. Each book I've read has fueled my voracious love for learning and unquenchable curiosity. Fiction transports me to different realms in just moments, while nonfiction exposes me to the complex world around.

Intrigued by the mysteries of faith and spirituality, I've also immersed myself in the study of many religions, investigating both their similarities and differences. This literary odyssey has fascinated me with how cultural and religious backgrounds shape our identities. I've analyzed and radically felt everything I've read, broken it down, compared perspectives, and purified what I've learned into common truths.

In all my professional roles, entrepreneurial ventures, personal experiences, and even in parenthood, one principle from my engineering training has consistently held true: every challenge can be reduced to its core formula, base understanding, lowest common denominator, or simple zero-one binary. Once identified, the next step is to distill this core principle and rebuild from that foundational level. This principle is universally applicable, offering clarity to solve any problem. I'll expand on this soon!

My unique blend of analytical and emotional intelligence, coupled with skills for pattern recognition, forms the cornerstone of my coaching methodology and what I apply in this book to alleviate anxiety. Simply: a system in which the engineer's mind meets the spiritual guide's heart and wisdom. Above all, my goal is to provide you with an avenue to nurture inner peace and harmony in all aspects of your life.

Writing this book has been deeply personal and fulfilling for me. While I always envisioned myself as an author, I never quite pictured my debut work centering around anxiety. Given such an eclectic background, why did I select anxiety as the subject of my debut book? Who am I to write a book on anxiety? I am a student of life who has evolved into a teacher by reading, inquiring, listening, feeling, and knowing.

Admittedly, anxiety is a term I've seldom used. My mind never truly accepted that label, despite my Four Bodies echoing the sentiments of "anxiety" throughout my life. Through my extensive work with individuals seeking relief from inner turmoil/pain and yearning for inner peace, the recurring theme of anxiety has been unmistakable. I've observed it as a universal language of distress that transcends all races, cultures, socio-economic backgrounds, genders, and ages. Phrases like "overwhelmed," "stressed," "struggling," and "anxious" arise time and time again.

It's key for me to highlight that I am not talking about anxiety disorders here. I am referring to the anxiousness, unease, overwhelm, stress, worry, angst, self-doubt, apprehension, restlessness, and even fatigue that plague all of us. I employ the term "anxiety" as a blanket term to capture each of these experiences.

It's time to move beyond this "anxiety" and live the life you desire. Are you with me?

I aim to present a fresh perspective by accentuating the importance of harmonizing The Four Bodies. This novel approach comes from integrating the analytical precision of my engineering background with the investigative insights of spiritual inquiry. When we master this harmony, we clear the way for a life devoid of overwhelm, fear, and limitations. I'll guide you towards a radiant life, equipping you with the skills necessary for achieving what I've termed "The Unconditional Three": Worthiness, Love, and Freedom.

I've sprinkled many Mattain terms, philosophies, and acronyms throughout the book, playfully referred to as "Mattain-Speak." A glossary is provided at the end of the book for your reference.

My teachings are arranged into a structured guide. Part I of this book focuses on rising above anxiety, while Part II addresses the transition from fear to freedom.

We'll examine strategies, tactics, and techniques, highlighting the stories of Julia, Pamela, Joanne, Karina, Alexa, Tony, Kevin, and others as examples showcasing the path towards the life you desire. The names in all case studies have been changed to protect privacy, and some details have been altered for clarity; however, the transformations represented are real, and I believe you'll find them quite inspirational.

You'll also be introduced to the pivotal Mattain Method, including my 5-4-3-2-1 Framework, The Mattain Five-Step Process, Deconstructing the Key Lime Pie Tool, and "The Antidote" to what I call "The Universal Fears."

While the method and tools are simple—as easy as 5-4-3-2-1—don't mistake this simplicity for a quick fix. Refining and continuously realigning with our infinite nature is a lifelong undertaking. As I fondly like to say, living completely pain-free (in the human sense) will only be truly achieved when we die. The concepts and stories I present will provide you with actionable ways to end mental turmoil, relieve pain, ease emotional distress, break free from limiting beliefs, and surrender to the present moment.

Part I lays the groundwork for Part II. Part I outlines The Four Bodies, the universal expressions of anxiety and fear, and how to achieve freedom, while

Part II equips you with the tools needed to do so. If you're eager to dive into the "how," feel free to fast-forward to Part II. However, I'd strongly encourage you to circle back to (or at least skim) Part I to fully grasp the fundamental aspects of our amazing human expressions through The Four Bodies and the human journey.

Note that throughout this book, certain unique elements of The Mattain Method, such as The Four Bodies and The Unconditional Three—along with others introduced later—are capitalized to show their significance within the framework. For further clarity on these terms and others, please refer to the glossary at the end of the book.

I applaud your being here, ready to confront any specific challenge or pattern that's holding you back from a life of genuine freedom. Together, we'll help you unearth the origins of your fears, reveal the wisdom they hold, and ultimately, break free from their constraints. Let's unravel your anxiety and fears to unveil your true essence.

My Love, Always.
Manal

PART I:
TRANSCENDING ANXIETY

Anxiety, simply, is unacknowledged fear of the future.

Welcome to Part I: Transcending Anxiety—here, we move beyond the label of "anxiety" and start listening to what our Four Bodies are truly telling us about fear and freedom.

This listening involves unraveling what we commonly call "anxiety." While the term is familiar, it's commonly misunderstood and overcomplicated. At its core, here's what we're really referring to when we talk about anxiety: *unacknowledged fear of the future.* As we develop greater awareness of the idea of unacknowledged fear of the future, we can learn to transcend the limitations that anxiety may impose on our lives.

Anxiety is undeniably a significant global concern. **Official figures show clinical anxiety disorders affect an estimated 284 million people worldwide, with numbers steadily increasing.[1] Global crises and significant events certainly amplify these conditions and their devastating impact.** The ripple effects can extend far beyond the individual, diminishing relationships, work productivity, and even physical health, sometimes preventing people from pursuing dreams and, indeed, from truly enjoying life.

Beyond these formal diagnoses, what many of us label "anxiety" in daily life is in many cases a complex mix. It can be that pervasive current of unease, fears about the future, the deep-seated need to control the uncontrollable, the relentless

---

[1] World Health Organization. "Mental Health and COVID-19: Early Evidence of the Pandemic's Impact: Scientific Brief." March 2, 2022. Retrieved from: https://www.who.int/publications/i/item/WHO-2019-nCoV-Sci_Brief-Mental_health-2022.1.

search for happiness, the pressure of "keeping up with the Joneses," or the weight of daily struggles, all intensified by everyday difficulties and overwhelm. This is something that touches virtually all of us. This broad, universal human experience of inner turmoil, rooted in deep longings and fears, is what we'll primarily explore in this book. These widespread resistant feelings, whether clinically defined or not, have the power to shape our existence, creating limitations on achieving true Worthiness, Love, and Freedom.

Within this book, we investigate how this ubiquitous experience—which I refer to as "anxiety"—exhibits in your multi-faceted self through your Four Bodies, with the ultimate goal of reclaiming your freedom.

As we proceed, you'll note that I emphasize the significance of doing more than just intellectual exercises. **Growth is not just about thinking; it is equally about believing, feeling, and being.** While reading a book can sometimes be perceived as a purely intellectual activity, I invite you to engage with this material on a deeper level. Let this book be more than just words on a page; let it be an experience that involves all your Bodies—Physical, Emotional, Mental, and Egoic—elevating your full, embodied awareness.

When you read about trust, self-compassion, love, and happiness, for example, strive to do more than just appreciate these virtues intellectually. *Feel them.* Allow them to resonate within you.

***Mattain Moment 1:* Mental vs. Emotional Happiness**

Let's try an experiment. Pause your reading for a moment.

1. **Think**: Say to yourself, "I should be happy right now." Notice how that feels in your mind and body. Is there effort? A subtle tension? A feeling of "trying?" Just observe the mental attempt to create happiness.

2. **Feel**: Now, let that thought go. Bring to mind someone or something that genuinely brings warmth to your heart—a loved one, cherished memory, or pet. Breathe into your heart space and simply welcome that feeling of joy or connection. Feel the ease.

Notice the difference? One is a mental assertion; the other is an allowing, a feeling that arises from within, centered in the heart. That embodied feeling *is* alignment.

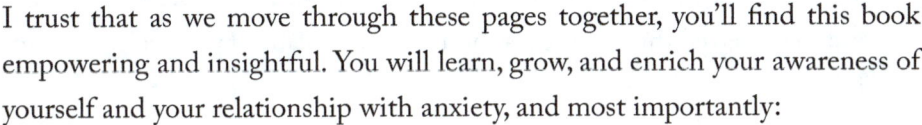

I trust that as we move through these pages together, you'll find this book empowering and insightful. You will learn, grow, and enrich your awareness of yourself and your relationship with anxiety, and most importantly:

You will transcend anxiety.

As we progress through the next few chapters, we begin a life-changing immersion together. You'll find understanding, acceptance, and, ultimately, freedom.

I define anxiety as *unacknowledged fears of the future*. These fears appear in Physical, Emotional, Mental, and Egoic expressions of The Four Bodies. In Part I, we'll bring to light your hidden fears, showing you how to release anxiety's grip and reclaim your emotional well-being. You'll discover how harmonizing your Four Bodies—Physical, Emotional, Mental, and Egoic—builds the foundation for a life of freedom and authenticity.

In Chapter 1, I'll discuss how societal expectations exacerbate these fears and how understanding them is the first step towards freedom.

Chapter 2 introduces The Mattain Four-Body Framework, where I share three kernels of wisdom that reveal the interconnectedness and intricacies of being human. Each of the following four chapters will zero in on one of The Four Bodies.

Chapter 3 focuses on the Egoic Body. We'll uncover how the fear of not being perfect can change how we see ourselves and how we act.

Chapter 4 details the Mental Body, examining how fears can lead to looping thoughts and feelings of being out of control.

In Chapter 5, we turn our attention to the Emotional Body, probing the responses and sensations associated with unacknowledged fears.

Chapter 6 brings us to the Physical Body, where we decode how our bodies respond to perceived threats. We also address the cascade of physical symptoms that follow.

In Chapter 7, we synthesize the content of the previous chapters, unveiling how all Four Bodies interrelate seamlessly, enabling us to proceed through life with flow, peace, and ease.

In the concluding sections of Part I, we learn alongside Pamela (a live session participant), bearing witness to her discovery of unrecognized emotions. Her story is enlightening, showcasing the swift and metamorphic power of facing and embracing our emotions, even when shadowed by unease and overwhelm. Her growth demonstrates an intimate perspective on the catalyzing influence of self-awareness and self-compassion.

Are you ready to bring awareness to your deeper patterns within? Let's welcome this unfolding into our authentic selves as we move beyond anxiety's constraints and fully embody unconditional Worthiness, Love, and Freedom.

SECTION I:
UNRAVELING THE NATURE OF ANXIETY

What we call "anxiety" is a coping mechanism, a disguise for the deeper, unexplored fears that truly drive our emotions.

CHAPTER 1
DEFINING ANXIETY

Anxiety is not the root cause, but a symptom, a surface label we use to avoid acknowledging the deeper fears within us.

Before we jump specifically into anxiety, it's important to understand the broader scope of this work. While "anxiety" is a central theme—because it's such a common term for the unease many experience—the principles and tools we'll explore are designed to address any form of discomfort or "resistance" that may be keeping you from a fulfilled life (more on "resistance" soon). These tools are universally applicable to the myriads of ways we can feel "off-kilter."

This discomfort, which we typically call anxiety or stress, stems from what I identify as unacknowledged fears. These fears can be induced for countless reasons. One may feel like the world is falling apart, politically, economically, or globally; indeed, this is not the first time in the history of humanity that things have felt hopeless for many.

But even if the wider world feels stable, our personal lives present constant opportunities to feel out of control, don't they?

Perhaps you're a "young pup," navigating the intense pressures of school, figuring out who you are and what path to take next. Or maybe you're in a mid-life transition, juggling career aspirations with evolving family dynamics, perhaps even finding yourself in that "sandwich" phase— lovingly caring for both children and aging parents. You might be moving through the significant transitions of marriage or divorce, building a new career, facing the quiet of an empty nest, or navigating the new landscape of retirement. And truly, regardless of our age or specific life stage, we all encounter challenges that can shake our sense of control: unexpected health issues (our own or a loved one's), financial uncertainties, the profound impact of loss, or the simple, undeniable truth that life doesn't always go according to our carefully laid plans. Or maybe you just plain 'ol identify with "anxiety," and that's perfectly okay, too.

Any of these external factors can make us feel like we're losing control. The truth is, anytime we primarily calibrate our well-being to the world around us, we risk feeling out of control because what's outside us is, by its very nature, unpredictable. This book will teach you how to calibrate internally through the alignment of your Four Bodies—Physical, Emotional, Mental, and Egoic—to connect with what I call The Unconditional Three: Worthiness, Love, and Freedom.

When we feel out of alignment with our inner truth, the resulting sensations can manifest as what many label anxiety, but also as struggle, suffering, disconnection, or general unease. Primary emotions like fear, anger, frustration, or even profound fatigue may surface in major ways.

This book, therefore, will teach you how to stop merely tolerating or reacting to the external world, and instead, start actively calibrating to the infinite beauty and power of your internal self.

So, while we'll focus significantly on "anxiety" as a common entry point, understand that we are truly addressing the roots of all such discomfort and resistance. Now, let's look further at how I define anxiety within The Mattain Method.

Regardless of its inciting event, what we call "anxiety" is, at its core, a collection of unacknowledged fears about the future. Millions worldwide share this forward-looking apprehension or dread of what may lie ahead. If this feeling resonates with you, rest assured that you're not alone.

But these fears show up as more than just a dread of the future. They arise within The Four Bodies, assuming various forms in daily life. We might experience them as worries about external factors like time, money, body image, and relationships, or as internal states like the fear of not being good enough, feeling out of control, or believing true happiness or love is unattainable. Let's see how these hidden fears reveal themselves.

The Emotional Whispers of Fear

Unacknowledged fears can be likened to a silent whisperer, subtly manipulating your emotional state. They can make you feel like you're on a perpetual roller-coaster of emotions, swinging between peaks of heightened worry and troughs of temporary relief. You may find yourself constantly on edge or note a lingering sense of unease. At times, these fears may even escalate into panic or terror, triggering a flood of intense emotions that feels overwhelming.

Mattain Moment 2: **Dominant Emotions**

Reflect on the most dominant emotions you've felt over the past week. Can you identify any recurring fears tied to these emotions?

Physical Manifestations: How Fear Resides in the Body

These fears don't just exist as emotions; they make themselves known in your body, too. When you're experiencing these fears, you might feel tense in your shoulders and arms, have a racing heart, upset stomach, headache, dry mouth, or tight jaw. These physical sensations are tangible, direct expressions of the underlying fear.

Mattain Moment 3: **Physical Manifestations of Fear**

Tune into your body right now. Are there areas of tension or discomfort? Take a moment to breathe into these areas and allow the sensations to simply be. Do you sense any shifts, perhaps relief, just through the simple act of holding these physical sensations in your awareness?

Mental Loops: The Thought Patterns of Hidden Fears

Unacknowledged fears overwhelm the mind, leading to looping thoughts, perceptions of being out of control, or sensations that something dreadful is imminent. You may feel like you're trapped on a runaway train, desperately seeking an exit but unable to find one.

Mattain Moment 4: **Looping Thoughts**

Reflect on your thought patterns over the past week. Have there been looping thoughts or persistent worries? Can you identify their origin?

Ego and Self-Perception: The Distortions of Fear

Within the Egoic Body, fears distort our self-perception, fostering self-defeating notions about our worth and wholeness. We might fixate on not meeting expectations (our own or perceived societal or familial ones) or feel gripped by a fear of losing control. This internal turmoil manifests as pervasive unease, dread, discomfort, or unhappiness, solidifying into persistent feelings of unworthiness—the belief that we're not good enough, smart enough, rich enough, thin enough, or attractive enough. These fear-driven narratives create barriers, obscuring our pathway to recognizing the Worthiness, Love, and Freedom that are inherently ours.

For example, when I became a mother, I found myself caught between two opposing expectations. On the one hand, society told me that being a good mother meant staying home and dedicating myself entirely to my children. On the other hand, there was pressure to pursue my career, achieve professional success, and be a financial contributor to the household. I felt torn between these two ideals, constantly questioning whether I was doing enough, being enough, for both my children and myself. This internal struggle stemmed from a fear of not being good enough, amplified by societal expectations and opinions.

During this period, I discovered I was very attached to both of these identities and let the roles of mother and professional define my worth. Until I connected with my unconditional, infinite worthiness, I wasn't able to move past these fears and cherish the fullness of my being, both as a mother and as a member of the workforce with unique passions and aspirations.

This process taught me the importance of recognizing and challenging limiting beliefs that arise from societal expectations and fears. It also revealed the radical power of connecting with our inherent worthiness and realizing that we are so much more than the roles we play or the expectations we try to meet.

Mattain Moment 5: **Not Enough-ness**

Think of a time when you felt unhappy, out of control, inadequate or "not enough." While you feel this sentiment internally, was there an external catalyst—an experience, message, or event—that might have fueled this misbelief?

Identifying the expressions of The Four Bodies for what they are—indications of unacknowledged fears—is crucial in discerning that they do not reflect your true worth as a person.

Acknowledging Fear: The Path to Liberation

Our society often rewards high achievers and glorifies "busyness," establishing a norm that we must constantly strive for perfection. This cultural expectation is further intensified by social media, where curated images of "ideal lives" are paraded and become the yardstick by which we measure our value. Our fears of inadequacy, of not being enough, earning enough, or producing enough, are heightened in an environment that ceaselessly demands more.

Once we become cognizant of these hidden fears, anxiety loses its power. The fears no longer lurk in the shadows, unidentified and controlling. They are brought into the light of our consciousness, ready to be seen, understood, and ultimately, transformed. This newfound awareness is the first step towards liberation and reclaiming your inner peace and happiness.

Understanding Resistance

Before we dig into the intricate ways in which these fears exhibit within our Four Bodies, it's timely to expand on a term that will weave throughout this book: "resistance."

Resistance refers to any obstruction or barrier within The Four Bodies that prevents us from alignment. Resistance manifests differently depending on its focus; feelings like guilt and shame typically relate to judgements about the past, whereas fear and anxiety generally stem from apprehensions about the future. Here's how resistance usually shows up in each of The Four Bodies:

- **Physical Body:** Resistance may present as pain, tension, or discomfort.

- **Emotional Body:** Resistance may take the form of anger, sadness, or frustration.

- **Mental Body:** Resistance could appear as limiting thoughts or judgements.

- **Egoic Body:** Resistance may emerge as misbeliefs or misconceptions about oneself and the world.

Acknowledging resistance in its numerous forms across The Four Bodies enables us to process the expressions of our unacknowledged fears with deeper intuition and empathy. I use the term "resistance" because what may express as fear to one person may feel like frustration to another. What may show up as "not good enough" to one may be expressed as "I am so dumb" to another. Using the broader term "resistance" allows us to normalize these diverse manifestations and prevents us from projecting one person's specific feeling onto another's. I invite you to pinpoint the specific ways resistance shows up in your Four Bodies.

Deconstructing the Term "Feeling"

Just as "resistance" helps us broadly categorize sensations of The Four Bodies, the word "feeling" is another term used loosely. Let's unpack this.

We tend to use "feeling" as a catch-all for our state of being, but this single word can represent the expressions originating from any of our Four Bodies. Understanding this concept allows for a potent expansion in self-awareness, because actively differentiating these expressions empowers you to scrutinize your experiences more accurately and address them more effectively at their root.

When you notice a "feeling," ask yourself: "Which Body is primarily speaking?" Recognizing the source helps immensely.

You'll notice that sometimes in this book, especially in open-ended prompts, I'll use the word "feeling" loosely in line with common English, trusting you to investigate the full spectrum of your experience. Other times, I'll intentionally ask about specific physical manifestations, emotional sensations, mental expressions, or egoic perceptions to guide you towards deeper clarity within your Four Bodies.

Mattain Moment 6: Unpacking the Word "Feeling"

Take a deep breath and check in with yourself right now. If someone asked, "How do you feel?", what might you say?

Notice how readily we use that word, "feeling." It's a common shortcut yet can represent perceptions from all of our Four Bodies, which makes it tricky to identify what's truly going on underneath. Let's break it down:

Physical Body Feelings (Sensations): You might say, "I feel tired," or "I feel tension here." These are primarily physical sensations.

Emotional Body Feelings (Emotions): You might say, "I feel happy," or "I feel anxious/sad/angry." These sentiments point to core emotions.

Mental Body Feelings (Thoughts/Beliefs): You might say, "I feel like this is the right decision," or "I feel confused." These expressions relay thoughts, judgements, or beliefs.

Egoic Body Feelings (Interpretations/Identity): You might say, "I feel misunderstood," "I feel inadequate," or "I feel like they don't care." These notions reflect interpretations of events related to our sense of self or how we relate to others.

Differentiating which Body is primarily speaking when you note a "feeling" is incredibly powerful for self-understanding. Doing so helps you address the true source of your experience.

Throughout the day, whenever you notice yourself saying or thinking "I feel..." just pause. Gently ask: "Which Body is this experience primarily coming from? Is this a physical sensation, a core emotion, a thought/belief, or an egoic interpretation?"

Don't judge, just notice. This practice sharpens your awareness across all Four Bodies.

In the following chapters, we'll dig further into the expressions of resistance, especially fears, within The Four Bodies. We'll investigate how our Four Bodies respond to perceived stressors, and the physical, emotional, mental, and egoic symptoms that follow. By understanding how The Four Bodies are interconnected, we can identify the root causes of resistance—which is the essential first step in learning how to release pain and anxiety and achieve greater well-being and a fulfilling life.

CHAPTER 2
RECOGNIZING ANXIETY IN THE FOUR BODIES

Anxiety, when it arises, does so in all Four Bodies—each Body holds its own form of resistance as it intermingles in the diverse fabric of our being.

As we discussed in the last chapter, anxiety doesn't show up in isolation. It's an intricate dance involving our physical sensations, emotional responses, mental processes, and egoic beliefs. Now, let's turn our attention to the interconnectedness of The Four Bodies and how these relationships can guide us towards overcoming overwhelm.

The Four Bodies: A Symphony of Self

Imagine your Four Bodies as instruments in an orchestra. The Physical Body is the percussion, grounding us in the tangible world through sensations and experiences. The Emotional Body is the strings, resonating with the full spectrum of human emotions. The Mental Body is the brass, providing structure and clarity through thought and processing. And the Egoic Body is the woodwinds, weaving the melody of our identity, beliefs, and ideologies.

When these instruments are in harmony, the music of our lives flows smoothly, creating a symphony of balance and well-being. However, when one instrument is out of tune, the entire orchestra is impacted, and the music becomes discordant. This is what happens when anxiety strikes—the harmony between The Four Bodies is disrupted, like an orchestra playing off key, resulting in a cacophony of distress.

Understanding this interplay is key. While this Four-Body framework offers a practical model, the idea that we are multi-layered beings resonates across diverse traditions. The multifaceted nature of humanity is a topic of interest in both Eastern and Western cultures. Incidentally, this theory of multiple bodies is not confined to any specific doctrine but is a synthesis of many, reflecting wisdom from a multitude of spiritual, religious, and philosophical sources.

Chronologically speaking, the notion that humans possess multiple dimensions or subtle bodies is ancient, appearing notably within the Hindu tradition. Early foundations can be traced back to the Upanishads (part of the Vedic scriptures), which described concepts like the five *koshas*—or sheaths—distinct layers of being.[2] Ideas about energy centers, or *chakras*, also emerged from these early roots. These concepts were later systematized in greater detail within subsequent Yogic and Tantric scriptures, which outline systems of seven primary chakras along the spine.[3]

Buddhist doctrine offers its own framework for the components of human experience through the Five Skandhas (aggregates), which include form (the physical body) alongside feeling, perception, mental formations, and consciousness.[4]

The major Abrahamic religions—Judaism, Christianity, and Islam—also hint at multi-dimensional aspects of human existence. In the 20th century, Western esoteric thinkers and New Age philosophers began to explicitly discuss these ideals, which have become further affirmed by contemporary

---

[2] Priya Paijwar, H. H. Awasthi, and Deepa Mishra, "Concept of Panchakosha in Vedic Literature." Banaras Hindu University, n.d., https://bhu.ac.in/Images/files/4-%20Priya%20Paijwar%2C%20H_%20H_%20Awasthi%20and%20Prof_%20Deepa%20Mishra.pdf.
[3] Parita Shah, "Chakras Explained: The Meaning, Origin & History of the Seven Chakra Vortexes," Parita Shah Healing, April 3, 2023. https://paritashahhealing.com/chakras-explained-meaning-origin-history/.
[4] Gaylon Ferguson, "How the Five Skandhas Build Our Sense of Self," Lion's Roar, March 11, 2020, https://www.lionsroar.com/how-five-skandhas-build-sense-self/.

holistic practices like Reiki, a healing technique that originated in Japan[5] and later became popularized in the United States.

Holistic practices address the Physical, Emotional, Mental, and Spiritual Bodies (I use Egoic instead of Spiritual—more on this soon). This model, commonly known in modern holistic medicine and psychology as PEMS, correlates in many aspects with my observations.

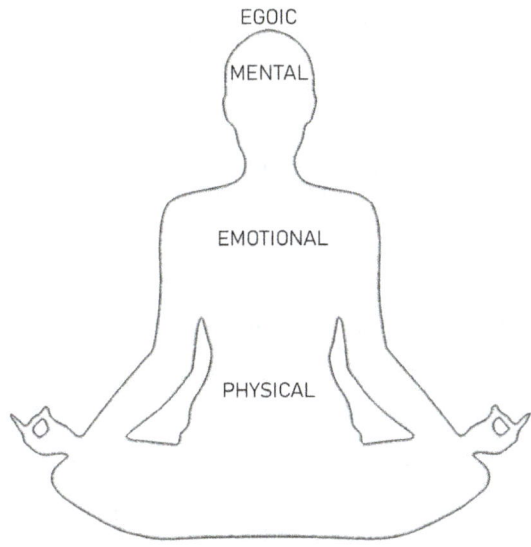

Figure 1: The Four Bodies

At times, I may list The Four Bodies from top to bottom: Egoic, Mental, Emotional, and Physical. Conversely, I may present them from bottom to top: Physical, Emotional, Mental, and Egoic. The order may be arbitrary or intentional, depending on the context and starting point of the impact.

In our current scrutiny of anxiety, we'll approach it top-down: starting with the Egoic Body and progressing to the Physical.

---

[5] Triplett, Stephanie. "Reiki." Encyclopædia Britannica, 2023. https://www.britannica.com/science/Reiki.

My Exploration of The Four Bodies

My understanding of The Four Bodies and their interconnectedness has evolved through intensive retreats, one-on-one coaching sessions, and personal breakthroughs.

In the following section, I'll share three pivotal revelations that have shaped my perspectives and informed the core teachings of my methodology.

- Revelation One: The Interplay of Physical Sensations, Emotions, and Memories

- Revelation Two: The Role of the Egoic Body

- Revelation Three: "It Just Is"

Revelation One: The Interplay of Physical Sensations, Emotions, and Memories

My first recognition of the interplay between the mind, emotions, and physical sensations emerged during a four-day retreat. At this event, a facilitator guided participants into introspection, enabling them to delve into their physical sensations, rooted emotions, and early memories. This process shed light on unconscious connections.

Let me share an example of this concept; it might seem surprisingly ordinary at first. Take the case of a participant we'll call Julia. She identified noticeable tension in her heart. When prompted to identify the emotion associated with this sensation, she instinctively responded with "profound sadness." Probing further led her to recall a childhood memory: being left alone by her parents for several days with a babysitter at around four years old. You may be thinking, "That doesn't sound so bad," but that's precisely the point. Even seemingly insignificant events, when experienced through the lens of a young child, can leave a lasting imprint.

This particular event left Julia feeling abandoned and unwanted. She also identified a deep-seated anger and resentment towards her parents, particularly her mother. Julia unwittingly carried this emotional narrative within her Four Bodies. We'll return to Julia's story later in this chapter to investigate how this presumably trivial event contributed to her larger patterns of anxiety and self-doubt.

Observing these unconscious holding patterns—intricate interplays between physical sensations, emotions, and early memories—was a recurring theme throughout the retreat. I noted that as participants shared and validated these ingrained narratives, they appeared to become lighter, as though long-carried burdens had been lifted. Identifying a pattern was a significant step towards healing and freedom from its grip. This epiphany was my first of many and became a stepping stone for deeper awakenings in the days, months, and years that followed.

While this revelation deepened my discernment of the links between emotions, body, and memories, it didn't reveal the ultimate truth that bridges our collective humanity. As I introduced earlier in the book, every challenge can be reduced to its root formula, base principle, and/or lowest common denominator. I sensed that there had to be something more. There had to be an equation showing that, despite race, age, gender, culture, and status, we're all the same.

In my pursuit to unearth this paradigm, I was led to discover a fourth Body: the Egoic Body. This evolving development was enriched by religious doctrines, global spiritual teachings, and perspectives from modern psychology, which reinforced my recognition of this critical fourth dimension.

Revelation Two: The Role of the Egoic Body

But what exactly is this "Egoic Body"—and why is it so essential to the framework I present? Often, when I encounter references to the "ego," they are framed in dismissive or even condescending terms. My thinking, stemming from the notion that every part of our nature has a purpose, led me to examine the more beneficial, even uplifting, aspects of the ego. I've come to see it as not just a reflection of our essence, but an embodiment of our core beliefs and identities.

Instead of viewing the ego as something negative that might be oppressive— becoming obnoxious and overbearing—or suppressed—remaining muted and unexpressed—I've come to see it as a bridge to spiritual connection, a conduit to something greater than ourselves.

When our Egoic Body harbors resistance, we take everything personally; this resistance blocks us from connecting to the spiritual state of oneness with all that is. When freed from resistance, the Egoic Body becomes a vehicle for accessing The Universal, The Divine.

Building upon this perspective, I realized the pivotal role of the ego when *aligned*. Reflecting on Julia's experience, I recognized it as a complex interplay across her Four Bodies: Physical, Emotional, Mental, and Egoic. Her narrative wasn't merely about being left alone; at its core was a belief formed in that vulnerable instance: I am at fault, I am unworthy, I am bad, I am unlovable, I am all alone. These deep-seated beliefs, born from a brief moment of sadness and confusion, had unknowingly shaped her emotional responses and physical sensations in adulthood.

Julia's recount illustrates a crucial concept: Early life events, particularly those involving loss, grief, or even supposedly minor events, perceived through a young mind can implant beliefs and misbeliefs about ourselves and the world. These perceptions, usually formed unconsciously, become the filter through which we engage wtih life, shaping our thoughts, emotions, and even physical well-being for years to come. The intensity of the emotional response may not always be consistent with the objective severity of the event, demonstrating the prominent role of early perception.

These inciting events (and their reactions) are commonly called "triggers," which can imply victimhood, so I prefer to see them as opportunities for deep self-awareness. By noticing the physical and emotional expressions in our bodies and approaching them with curiosity and a willingness to explore, we can begin to see how early conditioning contributes to these amplified responses.

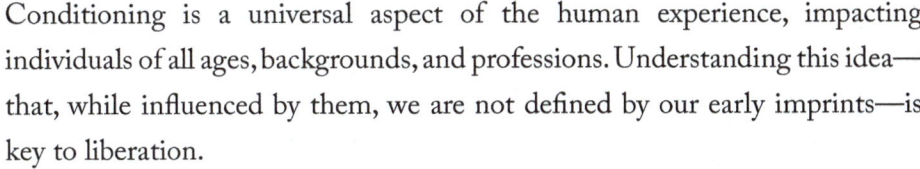

Mattain Moment 7: **Feeling "Triggered"**

Think about a time you felt "triggered." What earlier conditioning may have intensified your reaction?

Conditioning is a universal aspect of the human experience, impacting individuals of all ages, backgrounds, and professions. Understanding this idea— that, while influenced by them, we are not defined by our early imprints—is key to liberation.

In my coaching practice, I've witnessed this potency firsthand: teenagers struggling with self-doubt stemming from childhood bullying, seasoned professionals battling anxiety rooted in early career failures, and even elderly individuals grappling with physical ailments connected to unresolved grief. Each of these cases accentuates the significant impact of conditioning and the importance of identifying and addressing the underlying beliefs it creates.

As mentioned before, I propose a slight alteration in nomenclature from "Spiritual Body" to "Egoic Body." This refinement isn't a dismissal of the spiritual; instead, it acknowledges that the often misunderstood or oversimplified ego actually holds a significant place in our multi-dimensional humanness. The term "Spiritual Body" can inadvertently overlook the struggles, resistances, and tendencies we all grapple with. In popular perception, the Spiritual Body is frequently seen as infinite—a pristine realm untouched by human limitations and fallacies.

The Egoic Body, however, recognizes that these resistances—fears and misbeliefs—are an integral part of being human, and *through* them, not *around* them, we find our way to the spiritual. Therefore, "Egoic Body" feels more apt, as it acknowledges the very real presence of resistance and limiting beliefs within the same dimension that holds the capacity for spiritual connection. Releasing this resistance allows us to connect with The Divine, to feel oneness with life and all that is.

My aim is to weave these insights into a holistic framework for understanding our entire self. The Egoic Body is where we connect with specific labels and form our personal narratives. While in its resistant state, this Body can be a source of suffering, when freed from resistance, it becomes the very gateway to spiritual connection.

Now that we've explored The Four Bodies and their roles, it's time to consider something even more fundamental: the perspective that governs how we interpret our experiences. This brings me to my third major revelation—this one is less about a specific Body and more about a universal truth.

Revelation Three: "It Just Is"

Let's go back to Julia. What if I told you her parents left her not completely alone but with her grandparents because her mom was in the hospital giving birth to Julia's brother? This changes the plot, doesn't it? While Julia may instinctively want to blame her parents, the deeper insight here is that nobody is at fault; nobody is "bad."

"It just is."

Feel that for a moment. It's like releasing a heavy weight you didn't even know you were carrying. We're all interconnected in this intricate web of existence. Even if Julia's parents did something we'd quickly label as "bad," it's likely because her parents themselves were molded by their past experiences. Those who shaped our thoughts and behaviors were, in turn, influenced by their own past.

As I say in Mattain-Speak, "Our conditioners were conditioned, and their conditioners were conditioned."

Mattain Moment 8: **Your Conditioning**

Who conditioned you? Can you trace back your own web of influences? Do you find yourself blaming or feeling victimized by your conditioner(s)?

Here's the freeing part: Move away from a mindset of blame and appreciate that the unfolding of life is about self-realization and liberation. By embracing this perspective, we can release the tension, stress, and judgement we may be holding, creating space for ease, inner peace, and flow.

Can you feel the substantial freedom that comes with replacing the "bads" in your life with "It just is?" No one is bad. No one is wrong. Nothing is broken. This is just life.

I recognize that for some experiences, particularly those involving deep trauma, abuse, or profound loss, arriving at a place of "It just is" or immediate spiritual acceptance can feel incredibly difficult, perhaps even inappropriate. And that is perfectly okay. Your journey is uniquely yours. Often, individuals who have navigated unspeakable pain find their path towards alignment not necessarily through accepting the harmful act itself, but perhaps by recognizing the immense strength, resilience, or inner power they discovered within themselves because of that experience. Finding empowerment in your survival and growth is also a valid way to move towards surrender. This capacity for reframing and finding strength is a muscle, just like the others we are building throughout this book. The intention is always progress—moving along the spectrum towards greater alignment and peace, at your own pace, with deep self-compassion.

It's about accepting what is; not just intellectualizing it, but believing it, feeling it, and wholly embracing it within your Four Bodies.

Mattain Moment 9: Thinking vs. Feeling Acceptance

Let's highlight the difference between thinking and feeling acceptance.

1. **Think Acceptance (The "Should"):** Bring to mind a current struggle or challenge in your life—maybe at work, with family, or a personal habit—something you think you "should" accept but still feel resistance or unease around. Now, mentally tell yourself, "I accept this. It just is." Notice the effort involved. Does it feel forced? Do you hear an inner "But?" Where does resistance show up in your Physical Body (tension, tightness)? What underlying emotions are still present beneath the thought? What mental arguments arise? How does your Egoic Body feel (threatened, defensive, outraged)? Just observe this intellectual attempt at acceptance.

2. **Feel Acceptance (The "Is"):** Gently let that struggle go for now. Recall a past challenge, big or small, that you've genuinely made peace with. Something that no longer holds an emotional charge, that truly feels like "It just is (or was)." Connect with the feeling of that resolution. How does that acceptance feel in your Physical Body? Notice the ease, the relaxation. What is the emotional quality? Peace? Calm? Neutrality? Observe the quiet in your Mental Body. How does your Egoic Body feel? Surrendered? Complete? Connected?

Feel the difference? One is the mind *trying* to accept, layering over resistance. The other is an embodied state of peace, a true knowing that "It just is."

This feeling is where true freedom begins. It's an evolution from intellectual analysis to a felt sense of absolute acceptance, a resonance encompassing your entire being.

Here is another example of the reframe to "It just is." My editor recently shared her experience of being adopted. As a young girl and into early adulthood, she felt the deep pain of abandonment, the anger of being unwanted, and the ache of feeling unseen and unworthy. These victim thoughts implanted beliefs of not being good enough and unseen, manifested as visceral sensations in her body, and led to a constant source of emotional turmoil.

But in her thirties, forties, and beyond, she chose a different path. She chose acceptance—she recognized that her birth mom did the best she could and that resistant emotions like anger and sadness were not serving her. She validated her inherent worth, regardless of her life circumstances. This shift to acceptance softened the hold her emotions had on her and on her Four Bodies—Physical, Emotional, Mental, and Egoic. Now, she even enjoys a loving relationship with her birth mother, who has become one of her favorite people.

This is "It just is" in action.

When we stop blaming or running a victim mentality, we step into a place of empowerment. We free ourselves from the grip of negativity and open to the possibility of completeness and growth. This refinement of perspective allows us to genuinely feel the full spectrum of our experiences, leading to an amplified sense of contentment, peace, and wholeness. The inner void is filled, not by denying our emotions, but by embracing them with compassion and understanding. This is *radical acceptance*—a powerful catalyst for transformative liberation.

Mattain Moment 10: **It Just Is**

Think of a past event where you placed blame on yourself or others. You may have been running a program such as "I'm a victim," "So-and-so did me wrong," or "I'm not worthy/loved/free."

How does this sentiment change by feeling the situation through the lens of "It just is?"

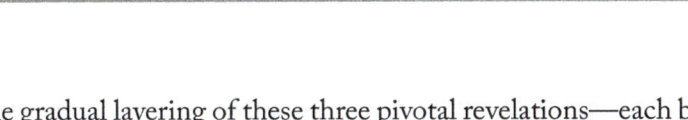

The gradual layering of these three pivotal revelations—each building upon the other—sparked a crystallization of my coaching methodology. My intuition evolved rapidly and in stages. Initially, I plunged into the complex interplay between physical sensations, feelings, and early childhood memories. Next, I came to pinpoint the deep-seated beliefs and misbeliefs that shape these elements. Subsequently, a key principle emerged: "It's no one's fault; It just is."

Putting the Three Revelations Together: The Path to "I AM"

These three revelations—the intricate interplay of our Physical, Emotional, and Mental Bodies, the dual nature of the Egoic Body, and the revolutionary power of "It just is"—are not separate insights, but interconnected steps on the path to wholeness.

They reveal a core truth: Life's occurrences, from the seemingly insignificant to the intensely impactful, leave imprints on all Four Bodies. These imprints, formed during the vulnerability of our developing minds, shape our beliefs about ourselves, our worthiness, our capacity for love, and our freedom.

The Egoic Body, in its resistant state, becomes the repository of these misbeliefs—the "I am not enough," "I am unlovable," and "I am trapped" narratives that fuel our fears and anxieties. But the Egoic Body, when freed from resistance, is also the gateway to our true nature, our connection to the universal.

The Mattain Method centers on radical acceptance: embracing the "It just is" of every situation, every thought, every emotion, every physical sensation. It's not about denying pain or pretending that everything is perfect. It's about acknowledging the full spectrum of human experiences, recognizing that every imprint, every belief, every feeling is a part of the whole.

The intention is not about thinking our way to acceptance; it's about feeling our way to peace.

This fundamental acceptance, embodied across all Four Bodies—felt in the Physical, acknowledged in the Emotional, trusted in the Mental, and integrated in the Egoic—allows us to dissolve limiting beliefs and align with Worthiness, Love, and Freedom. It allows us to just *be*. This is the path to "I AM"—not as a concept, but as a lived reality. This "I AM" is the elemental state of being that exists beneath all identities, roles and labels we adopt, such as "parent," "sibling," "friend," "student," "professional," etc. It is simply pure existence: "I AM"—period.

Through this book, my goal is to guide you in identifying and honoring all facets of your being. Seeing and valuing the unique expressions of your Four Bodies and the imprints they carry leads you to harmonize them, unlocking your innate capacity for a life of joy, peace, abundance, and connection. When your Four Bodies are in sync, your true self—whether you refer to it as your soul, spirit, or inner light—shines radiantly. I call this harmonious state "alignment."

Returning to our discussion on anxiety, paying attention to how it shows up in The Four Bodies is essential. By identifying these signs—physical tensions, racing thoughts, suppressed emotions, limiting beliefs—we can begin to address and, ultimately, release them. The aim is not to identify with these symptoms, but to recognize them as signals, guiding us towards underlying issues that need our attention.

The following chapters will deconstruct the manifestations of anxiety in the Egoic, Mental, Emotional, and Physical Bodies, respectively (from top to bottom).

CHAPTER 3
UNDERSTANDING ANXIETY IN THE EGOIC BODY

Anxiety can show up in the Egoic Body as being a perfectionist, judging yourself as imperfect, feeling unworthy, or fearing that you're not good enough.

We now turn to the "Egoic Body," the home of our core beliefs and the lens through which we identify with stress and unease. Within this Body lie our identity, beliefs, and misbeliefs about ourselves, our lives, and the world. This Body is also the home of our desires for control and freedom, elements which influence our unacknowledged fears about the future.

Both our need for control—be it over life, ourselves, or others—and pursuit of freedom are intimately tied to fear. When we believe we are bad, life is wrong, a lack of meaning is present, freedom is elusive, or feel like we're losing control, these fears surface, giving rise to what we perceive as anxiety. Ultimately, transcending the limitations of the ego is the portal to the spiritual, allowing us to become one with life.

In this chapter, we'll further uncover the role of the Egoic Body, introduce The Unconditional Three, and reveal how The Egoic Body expresses The Universal Fears.

Understanding the Egoic Body

The Egoic Body is the seat of our identity and core beliefs, shaped from birth by factors such as gender, nationality, religion, and culture. While these identities connect us to external realities, it is through exploring them—understanding both their value *and* their limitations—that we are pointed towards a universal truth: the realization of "I AM." This essence encompasses our purpose, value, and worth, independent of any specific external identity.

In the Egoic Body, we strike a balance between individual circumstances and a universal connection to higher energies and meaning.

Due to societal conditioning and our early background, the Egoic Body directs us towards external factors, casting our experiences in a narrative of struggle and victimhood. However, life's underlying architecture also provides internal cues for meaningful realignment. By acknowledging these cues and adjusting our beliefs to orient to "I AM," our limited mindset is elevated to one of limitless potential.

The ultimate purpose of life is to guide us from external identification to internal calibration of our intrinsic truth. This transition not only frees our thoughts and emotions but also positively impacts all Four Bodies. My teachings aim to facilitate this fundamental reframe, reinforcing the idea that life is a beautiful, mysterious, and expansive opportunity.

The Unconditional Three

We are in a lifelong pursuit of The Unconditional Three. They are, in my view, the basic qualities of our true nature, what we connect with when the ego's resistance dissolves. They are the essence of "I AM"—the wholeness that exists before any conditioning, beyond any fear.

Throughout this book, I will refer to these qualities—Worthiness, Love, and Freedom—as The Unconditional Three. Our collective aim is to align with The Unconditional Three; occasionally, I'll highlight this objective using the term "unconditional" before Worthiness, Love, and Freedom. The word "unconditional" reflects the intention that these states are to be embodied without any restrictions, limitations, or conditions—fully and completely.

While these terms have been chosen for clarity and consistency, they represent constructs far more significant than their straightforward meanings suggest.

THE UNCONDITIONAL THREE

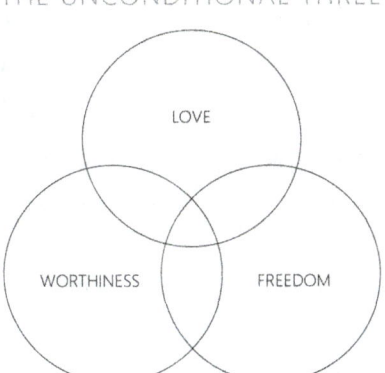

Figure 2: The Unconditional Three

- **"Worthiness"** is the recognition of our inherent value and belonging, a genuine connection to the world that naturally fosters confidence, belonging, self-acceptance, and self-compassion.

- **"Love"** is unconditional happiness, joy, inner peace, and contentment. It's a state of being that exists independent of external circumstances or expectations. While many have experienced love relationally with distortions, conditioned by expectations to conform, to be "good," or to follow predetermined trajectories, true love transcends these limitations. We don't need to seek love or strive to be loved: We *are* love.

- **"Freedom"** is the experience of non-duality: the realization that there is no true separation between us and The Universe. It's a state of complete openness, where the boundaries of the ego dissolve, and we unlock infinite liberation. In this state, we think and believe as we choose, and we feel the full spectrum of human emotion without resistance. When we embody complete inner freedom, our experience of life becomes expansive and unbound. This state is the ultimate goal of the spiritual path: to move beyond the illusion of separation and recognize our oneness with all that is.

If the terms "Worthiness," "Love," and "Freedom" resonate with you in their purest forms, I invite you to embrace them fully. However, I recognize that these words can be loaded, and past encounters might have distorted their meaning. If you find yourself resisting any of these terms, or if they don't quite capture the feeling(s) you're seeking, I encourage you to use your own language.

- Perhaps, instead of Worthiness, you connect more deeply with a sense of belonging, deservingness, self-acceptance, inherent value, self-love, or simply feeling good enough.

- Perhaps Love, for you, is better defined as inner peace, joy, contentment, unconditional acceptance, compassion, connection, oneness, or harmony.

- And perhaps Freedom feels more like liberation, spaciousness, openness, non-attachment, release, flow, or authenticity.

I've structured my discussion around Worthiness, Love, and Freedom and their corresponding fears in this specific order for consistency. However, please note that there's no hierarchy among them. Each element holds its own importance, and you may find yourself connecting with different desires at various stages of your growth. The sequence I present moves from the physical expressions of life to deeper, existential aspects, offering a natural and introspective progression. The beauty and mystery of the amazing human experience lie in the lifelong process of recalibrating to the fundamental truths of our Worthiness, Love, and Freedom (The Unconditional Three).

We are conditioned to seek these attributes externally until life presents us with moments that lead us to realize The Unconditional Three reside within us. They always have and always will.

Anxiety and fear serve as valuable guides which lead us inward introspectively, as exemplified by your decision to read this book. However, the resistant Egoic Body holds deep fears that block our connection to The Unconditional Three.

The Universal Fears

In the context of rising above anxiety, let's now look at three universal fears found within the resistant Egoic Body. By acknowledging these fears, we begin to loosen their hold on our lives and emancipate ourselves from the grips of inner turmoil.

- *The fear of inadequacy* (not enough) is the opposite of inherent Worthiness.

- *The fear of never achieving love* is the opposite of unconditional Love.

- *The fear of uncertainty* is the opposite of infinite Freedom.

These fears, in essence, are distorted reflections of our deepest desires. They point us, however indirectly, towards what we truly long for: to be worthy, to be love, and to be free.

This realization allows us to consciously "Flip the Script." Even before dissecting each fear, we can begin asking: "What is the opposite of the fear I'm feeling? What is the desired state—Worthiness, Love, or Freedom—that this fear is guiding me towards?" This inquiry shifts our focus from the unwanted to the desired.

1. Fear of Inadequacy and/or Unworthiness

Our Egoic Body is where we form our perceptions of worthiness and where we constantly evaluate ourselves, our actions, and our worth based on the standards set by society and/or ourselves. We tend to compare our lives and accomplishments to others', leading to feelings of inadequacy and unrecognized fears about our worthiness. It's important to note that everyone's life is unique and cannot be compared. Yet a resistant Egoic Body often overlooks this idea, leading to unease.

Mattain Moment 11: **Connecting with the Fear of Not Enough**

Take a deep breath and turn your awareness inward with curiosity. Now, invite the feeling of being "not good enough" or inadequacy into your present awareness. Investigate how it feels, and simply welcome its presence for this exploration, observing it without judgement.

What is the specific "flavor" or dominant texture of this "not enough" feeling? Tune into your Physical Body: where does this feeling live? Is there a tightness in your chest, a knot in your stomach, a weakness in your knees, perhaps even nausea? Does it manifest as a deep sense of unworthiness? Does it show up as anxious perfectionism? Does it lead to patterns of self-sabotage? Or is it primarily a gripping fear of failure or judgement? Allow your curiosity to open your awareness.

For now, can you just be with this texture or flavor, observing it simply as a pattern or expression that arises within your human setting?

2. Fear of Never Achieving Love or Lasting Happiness

The Egoic Body's struggle doesn't end there. It's constantly in pursuit of happiness, love, peace, joy, or what some may call the "ultimate state of being." Yet the road it typically takes to achieve this state is riddled with hidden fears. The search for these states can feel like an endless chase. The more we seek them, the more elusive they become.

Mattain Moment 12: **Holding the Fear of Seeking Love**

Take a breath and connect with the deep desire to find love, be loved, or for lasting love, peace, or happiness. Gently invite awareness of any underlying fear that you may never truly achieve these states. What is the specific "flavor" or physical sensation of this fear within you?

For this moment, simply observe this fear with curiosity, recognizing it as part of the Egoic Body's seeking pattern, without needing to resolve it.

3. Fear of Uncertainty or Loss of Control

One of the primary struggles we face, sometimes described as originating in our "Egoic Body," is the fear of the unknown and the accompanying loss of control. We inhabit an unpredictable world where we cannot control life or death. As a result, our ego yearns for predictability and seeks to exert control as a means of feeling secure.

The essential nature of this human journey—the "game of life"—is uncertainty about what tomorrow holds. Yet, paradoxically, existing *within* this very uncertainty is our key to unconditional Freedom.

Herein lies a crucial point of confusion: Driven by a desire to *experience* our true freedom, we mistakenly try to achieve it by controlling the uncontrollable. We attempt to manage external circumstances, futures, or others, believing our actions will grant us the feeling of freedom we seek. However, when these efforts inevitably fall short against the backdrop of life's unpredictability, our unacknowledged fears of uncertainty surface, triggering anxiety.

True freedom lies not in controlling the external, but in how we relate to the uncertainty itself: through surrender, flow, and allowing.

Mattain Moment 13: **Allowing Flow Amidst a Fear of Uncertainty**

Take a breath and bring to mind an area in your life currently filled with uncertainty or where you feel a distinct lack of control.

Notice the sensations that arise in your body—perhaps tightness, bracing, or an urge to manage the unknown. What is the "flavor" of this fear of losing control or facing the unknown?

Gently acknowledge this response as the Egoic Body's natural pattern: seeking security by trying to control the irrefutably uncontrollable nature of life.

Just for this moment, breathe into that feeling. Can you simply be aware of both the uncertainty and the desire for control, recognizing that true freedom lies in allowing? What would it feel like to simply embrace allowing and flow in these areas?

Due to their many forms and nuanced expressions, I refer to these primary fears collectively as "The Universal Fears."

The first step towards liberation is bringing these fears into awareness; this is a whole-being experience, engaging your Egoic, Mental, Emotional, and Physical Bodies. By recognizing these fears as expressions of limiting beliefs, not fundamental truths, we begin to release their grip on The Four Bodies.

What do we move towards when we release these fears? The answer can be found in the opposites: what is the opposite of the fear of inadequacy, the opposite of the fear of being unlovable (or never finding love), and the opposite of the fear of uncertainty (or loss of control)? The Unconditional Three: Worthiness, Love, and Freedom. As we release the grip of these fears, we naturally open ourselves to these states of being.

Mattain Moment 14: **Seeing Your Fears**

Consciously use your breath to connect with your Four Bodies—Physical, Emotional, Mental, and Egoic. Breathe in deeply and with intent. Pause for a moment with your lungs full, noticing the stillness of your breath. Then, gently release the breath, exhaling slowly and completely. Notice the quiet stillness again in the pause when your lungs are empty, just before your next inhale begins. Feel how this mindful cycle connects you.

With renewed clarity and purpose, shape your intention. From this moment, commit to transforming your "unacknowledged" fears into "seen" fears. These fears now stand apparent, shining brightly in your consciousness, owing to your steadfast intention to recognize, honor, and even welcome them with love. With compassion, absorb yourself in this introspective moment, seeing the many facets of your fears, whether you encounter newfound realizations or ongoing paths in your self-exploration.

As you draw in another breath, feel the sensation of air filling your lungs. With this breath, ignite a keen awareness of each of your Four Bodies: Physical, Emotional, Mental and Egoic. And as you exhale, let go of the weight of old conditioning. Feel a sense of spaciousness and openness. Now, welcome and smile at each of your Four Bodies, embracing them without judgement, celebrating them in all their current states. You may wish to give them each a hug, have a group hug, or welcome them in another way, perhaps with words, a playful high five, or a bow. You may welcome them all in the same way, or you may adjust your welcoming words and acts to suit each Body.

Linger in this moment. Whatever you see, hear, feel, or sense is just perfect. Focus on your breath and your Four Bodies and bask in your intention to release whatever was holding them back, recognizing the importance of each individually and their integration with one another. Recalibrate whatever needs adjusting. Welcome your fears in their true essence, appreciating the strength of this moment.

As you complete this exercise, notice any changes in your state. Do you feel a sense of greater ease? Inner peace? Connection? Excitement? These are glimpses of your unquestionable Worthiness, Love, and Freedom.

When you feel balanced and prepared, progress forward.

Flip the Script: Connecting Fear to Your Desired State

Now that we've explored The Universal Fears and practiced seeing them with awareness, let's revisit the "Flip the Script" questions more deeply. Reflect: "What is the opposite of this fear? What is the desired state I'm truly seeking?"

This conscious shift is incredibly powerful for reclaiming your alignment. Here's how it maps out:

- If you notice fears related to inadequacy, perfectionism, comparison, or failure: Ask, "What is the opposite?" The answer points towards your desire for inherent Worthiness. You can then ask, "How can I connect with my unconditional Worthiness?"

- If you notice fears related to finding happiness, being alone, feeling rejected, or being unlovable: Ask, "What is the opposite?" This reveals your desire for Love (in its broadest sense, including happiness, joy, connection, peace). You can then ask, "How can I connect with the Love that I already am?"

- If you notice fears related to uncertainty, needing to control outcomes, feeling trapped, or the unknown (even death): Ask, "What is the opposite?" This uncovers your desire for Freedom (inner liberation, flow, trust, surrender). You can then ask, "How can I embrace my Freedom in this moment?"

This practice moves you from analyzing fear to actively calibrating towards The Unconditional Three.

Within the Egoic Body, our reality synchronizes with our belief system. If our beliefs are dominated by fear and anxiety, our reality will reflect the same. When they are calibrated to unconditional Worthiness, Love, and Freedom, our reality will reflect this. And remember the very first quote I shared: "It's hard, until it's not."

The Egoic Body's non-resistant state embodies The Unconditional Three: Worthiness, Love, and Freedom, propelling us towards an infinite, authentic connection with self, life, and beyond.

The lifelong intentions of acknowledging, processing, and releasing the fears that are the opposite of The Unconditional Three is incredibly rewarding. The goal is to not just alleviate the symptoms of anxiety but to *fully embody The Unconditional Three*. This metamorphosis is a beautiful, ongoing opportunity for self-discovery and empowerment.

So far, we've discussed the role of the Egoic Body in our experiences of anxiety, considered the significance of identity, beliefs, and conditioning in shaping this Body, examined three core fears that reside within it, and introduced the catalytic powers of The Unconditional Three. In the next chapter, we'll examine the Mental Body and its relationship with anxiety.

CHAPTER 4
UNDERSTANDING ANXIETY IN THE MENTAL BODY

Mental symptoms of anxiety can include looping thoughts, feeling out of control, or fearing that something dreadful is about to happen.

To understand and overcome anxiety, we turn to the Mental Body—where our thoughts, interpretations, and perceptions shape our reality. The Mental Body, when in balance, acts as a powerful ally; however, when it's out of balance, it can become a significant source of stress. At times, the Mental Body falls prey to the "monkey mind," a restless state marked by incessant, circling thoughts that ensnare and disturb us.

The Mental Body is a dynamic processor, powering our thinking, goal setting, and self-expression. It's the seat of logic and reason, a potent tool for navigating the world. But life is more than just logic; it's also about emotion, intuition, and experience.

Intellectualizing Life: The Balance of Mind and Emotion

To intellectualize life is to seek logical explanations for all our encounters.

The mind excels at logic and analysis. I get it. I'm an engineer, remember? But while logic is valuable, life is a tapestry of emotions, serendipities, and nuances that can't always be refined into rational thought. By incessantly trying to analyze and make sense of everything, we rob ourselves of the spontaneous joys and surprises that life offers.

For instance, picture a child laughing uncontrollably at a silly joke. Do you join in their laughter, feeling the infectious joy and lightness of the moment? Or do you overanalyze the humor and question its intellectual merit, thereby missing the opportunity to connect with the pure, unadulterated jubilance of the child?

Conversely, consider when something challenging occurs—perhaps a sudden setback like a missed flight, unexpected injury, or even a significant life change like a divorce. The mind can spin endlessly, trying to intellectually understand why it happened, replaying events, searching for a logical cause or someone to blame. I've spent my share of time in that mental loop! But I eventually realized I might never find a neat, intellectual answer for some of life's toughest moments. The real shift, the real peace, came when I stopped demanding to understand and instead chose to trust—to lean into the awareness that these difficult experiences ultimately lead to incredible growth, inner strength, and a deeper alignment with my personal power. Staying stuck in the "why" robbed me of seeing those gifts... until I was able to break free.

Over-intellectualizing can lead to feelings of detachment, where we become observers of life rather than active participants. We miss out on the intangible essence of being human—the magic, the vibrancy, the depth and richness of emotionally charged moments. When we try to make sense of everything, we inadvertently strip away the very qualities that make life meaningful.

The same principle applies to practices like gratitude. It's one of my spiritual peeves when gratitude becomes an intellectual exercise—a "should" based on what we think we ought to feel, rather than a genuine expression of appreciation. True gratitude is a full-body experience, a felt sense of thankfulness that arises naturally when we are present and connected. It's not about forcing ourselves to be happy or ignoring our other emotions; it's about allowing ourselves to let appreciation fill us from the inside out.

Expressions in the Mental Body consists of perceptions and attitudes. A resistant mind is like a closed fist, tightly gripping opinions and prejudices, unable to open to new ideas.

Anxiety in the Mental Body

What happens when our interpretations are skewed by fears? Fears about the future and the drives for control, freedom, and happiness all translate into anxiety in the Mental Body.

One characteristic of anxiety in the Mental Body is looping thoughts or chronic worry. It's like being stuck on a hamster wheel of fear, constantly going round and round without any real progress or resolution. These looping thoughts are frequently characterized by "what if" scenarios; you may be endlessly assessing potential outcomes and trying to predict what will happen next. This exhausting and futile struggle leaves us drained and overwhelmed.

When overwhelm takes hold, we can fall into the trap of believing that if we think hard enough or worry enough, we'll somehow be able to control future events. This perception is a fallacy that only serves to fuel our anxiety further. Our Mental Body resists life's unpredictability in its search for control. This resistance creates the feeling of losing control, which then triggers further anxiety.

When consumed by fear, the Mental Body can also distort our perceptions of reality. This distortion can take many forms, from overestimating the likelihood of negative outcomes to underestimating our ability to cope with different situations. This distorted thinking can create a negative feedback loop, thereby reinforcing our fears and magnifying our anxiety.

The Mental Body also shapes our self-image, reflecting our self-worth from the Egoic Body. When our worthiness is in question, doubts can permeate our Mental Body, creating a state of constant unease and self-doubt, another breeding ground for anxiety.

More than the Mind: The Integrated Roles of The Four Bodies

In understanding anxiety, we must become conscious of its interconnected nature and not view it as an array of isolated symptoms. Anxiety doesn't exist in a vacuum; it's intensely tied to our behaviors, desires, thought patterns, and fears. Each of these aspects is processed and reflected in our Four Bodies.

We tend to blame the mind for our anxiety and our inability to control our thoughts. However, we must comprehend that *the mind is processing for all Four Bodies.*

The mind interprets signals not only from its own cognitions but also from our Physical, Emotional, and Egoic Bodies. Therefore, what we perceive as anxiety in our Mental Body is, in fact, an indication of underlying dynamics across all Four Bodies.

It's easy to see how your beliefs directly impact your thoughts, which in turn impact your emotions, and ultimately guide your actions.

Consider the example of going for a job interview. If you hold the belief that you're qualified and capable, your thoughts will likely be along the lines of: "I'm excited to show them what I can bring to this role." This thought evokes emotions of confidence and enthusiasm, which result in actions like presenting yourself assertively in the interview via both body language and a strong voice.

Conversely, if your belief is that you're not good enough for the job, your thoughts may be filled with dread, such as "I'm going to mess this up." This thought triggers anxiety and fear, leading to nervous behavior and stumbling over your words.

Can you see from this example that the mind is not always the root source of anxiety? *Underlying beliefs, rather than mere thoughts, drive anxiety.* These beliefs set off a chain reaction; they channel our thoughts, spark our emotions, and ultimately guide our behavior and outcomes.

When things don't go as planned, we might instinctively fault our mind. However, it's our foundational beliefs, held in our Egoic Body, that mold those thoughts which empower or limit us.

This relationship underscores the deep interconnections between our beliefs (trust), thoughts (knowledge), emotions (feelings), and actions (doing).

Whether these beliefs are right or wrong, they undeniably have a concerted impact on our thoughts, feelings, and actions. Grasping this interconnected influence is vital. We shouldn't attribute our actions or emotional states solely to our minds. Rather, we must understand the complex dance between The Four Bodies that defines our experiences.

How frequently do you catch yourself placing blame on only your thoughts or mind for your feelings and actions?

Recognizing such a pattern can help us become cognizant of the complexities of anxiety and how it materializes. By witnessing these connections, we can start to unravel anxiety's underlying roots and address it in a more holistic, effective way.

Mattain Moment 15: **Thoughts & Core Beliefs**

Let's begin by exploring your relationship with your mind. With curiosity and openness, take a moment to reflect: How do you generally feel *about* your mind? Are there judgements you hold about it? Perhaps frustration with uncontrolled looping thoughts, feelings of self-doubt, labels like "ADD," "forgetful," "slow learner," "stupid," or "crazy?"

Becoming aware of these judgements and patterns regarding your mind is crucial.

Next, anchor yourself with a deep inhale and exhale.

Now, instead of placing focus or blame solely on your thoughts, recognize that these mental habits stem from deeper core beliefs held in your Egoic body.

What foundational belief, tied to your sense of Worthiness, Love, or Freedom, could be the source driving the frustration, self-doubt, or control patterns you just observed? Consider feeling inadequate or "not good enough" [Worthiness], fearing rejection, isolation, or being unworthy of connection [Love], or needing to rigidly control outcomes or not feeling truly free [Freedom].

Simply acknowledge the powerful link between these underlying beliefs and your mental landscape.

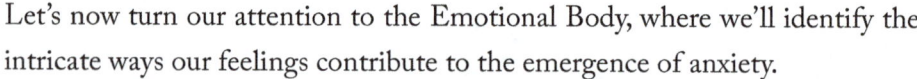

Let's now turn our attention to the Emotional Body, where we'll identify the intricate ways our feelings contribute to the emergence of anxiety.

CHAPTER 5
UNDERSTANDING ANXIETY IN THE EMOTIONAL BODY

Often, we use anxiety as an excuse to avoid investigating our genuine emotions.

The Emotional Body plays a pivotal role in anxiety; it serves as the reservoir of unexpressed fears, the dam holding back a rush of unacknowledged emotions. Anxiety, at its core, is the outcome of these emotions and their resulting feelings, which we dare not voice or even admit to ourselves.

I consider the Emotional Body as the command center of our Four Bodies. As we discussed in the last chapter, many of us have been conditioned to rely mainly on our Mental Body, traveling through life with logic, goal setting, and intellect. However, work, relationships, learning, and life become so much easier and more pleasurable when infused with passion, compassion, inspiration, desire, and love—all expressions from the Emotional Body.

Before we continue, let's clarify a subtle yet important distinction used throughout this work: the difference between *emotions* and *feelings*. Emotions originate in the Emotional Body; they are the basic vibrational energies we emit—core signals like fear, joy, sadness, or anger. Feelings, on the other hand, are the ways we perceive and experience these underlying emotions. They manifest primarily as physical sensations in the Physical Body (like a tightness in the chest associated with sadness) or as thoughts and interpretations arising in the Mental or Egoic Body (like worried thoughts linked to fear).

So, think of emotion as the energy source, and feeling as its perceived expression or sensation. Understanding this distinction helps us traverse our inner landscape with greater precision.

When you harness your Emotional Body, allowing your heart's wisdom to take the lead, your Mental thoughts, Physical actions, and Egoic beliefs are guided naturally. This heart-centered alignment is where true gut instinct, intuition, and inspired action arise, signaling that you've tapped into a wisdom far greater than the analytical mind alone. This is how you unlock a life of authentic creativity, easeful flow, and profound alignment.

Honoring Your Emotions

So how do we arrive at this state of harmony and flow? The key lies in attentively listening to, appreciating, accepting, respecting, honoring, and even loving your emotional feedback system unconditionally.

Note that these terms—listening, appreciating, accepting, respecting, honoring, and loving—are not reserved solely for the positive and wanted experiences of life; they also extend to the experiences perceived as unwanted.

But how can we honor, respect, or love the challenging aspects of life, the so-called "negatives?" Many of us lean towards feelings that make us feel good and shy away from (or suppress) the uncomfortable ones.

What if we treated *all* emotions as feedback? What if anger is a signal pointing us towards our deepest desires? Could fear be a mechanism designed to keep us safe? Or sadness a compass pointing us to what we want? By discerning the value of each emotion, respect and honor naturally follow. Over time, this understanding can even evolve into love.

Consider the seatbelt alarm in your car. This warning system, a mix of lights and beeping, reminds you to buckle up. While it can be seen as an annoyance, especially if you're momentarily choosing not to buckle up, its primary purpose is to ensure your safety. Recognizing this protective intent leads us to respect and perhaps even honor it. In a critical situation, moreover, it becomes something we appreciate and even love.

Emotions as a Coping Mechanism: Understanding "PAINS"

Similarly, our emotions act as inborn feedback mechanisms. Naturally, we gravitate towards states like joy and peace, while sometimes resisting emotions like anger or sadness.

It's intriguing to observe how many of us are conditioned to harbor resentment towards our "negative" emotions—anger, sadness, grief, frustration, and fear, among others.

Much of the pain associated with our emotions arises not from the feelings themselves, but from the judgements and resistance we associate with them. I refer to this concept as "resistance on resistance."

Mattain Moment 16: **Bubbling Emotions**

Take a moment to tap into how you feel when you're anxious. What emotions bubble to the surface? Are they clear and identifiable, or is there a murky mix of dread, worry, and unease?

More often than not, we don't permit ourselves to fully experience our emotions and their resulting feelings/sensations. We resist acknowledging them, which in turn, strengthens their grip on us. We cloak these emotions in the ambiguity of anxiety rather than face them head-on.

We commonly resist our emotions in five ways, a process summed up in Mattain-Speak with the acronym PAINS.

P: Projecting

A: Amplifying

I: Intellectualizing

N: Negating

S: Suppressing

Projecting involves deflecting our emotions onto others, diverting our attention away from self-reflection. For instance, feeling angry but accusing someone else of being hostile, or feeling self-critical but constantly finding fault in others' actions.

Amplifying is the act of overstating or exaggerating our emotional reactions, which can create further emotional turmoil in the long run. This could sound like turning a minor inconvenience into a catastrophe ("This traffic jam is the WORST thing ever!") or magnifying a small hurt ("That comment totally ruined my whole day!").

Intellectualizing is when we explain away our feelings, focusing on viewing them logically rather than experiencing them. "First-world problems" and "I should be thankful" are two common statements that intellectualize one's experience.

Negating involves invalidating or denying our emotions, telling ourselves we shouldn't feel a certain way, thereby avoiding our true emotional state. This commonly sounds like saying "I'm fine," "I'm okay," or "It's not a big deal" when we actually feel upset or distressed. This pattern can even extend outward, such as when we negate another's feelings by telling them "You're okay" when they are clearly expressing pain or sadness.

Suppressing is the conscious or unconscious act of avoiding or burying our emotions, a tactic that might provide temporary relief but could lead to significant emotional or physical health problems if these emotions are not eventually addressed. Suppressing often involves "stuffing down" feelings, quickly changing the subject when things get uncomfortable, staying overly busy to avoid introspection, or physically holding tension in the body (like a tight jaw or shallow breath) to keep emotions at bay.

The defensive mechanisms represented by PAINS are common yet unhelpful strategies, and we may even be combining more than one. Even if they temporarily shield or distract us from discomfort, these unhealthy patterns prevent us from processing our emotions. These coping strategies may keep the dam from breaking, but they don't address the water itself.

The pressure builds as the unrecognized emotions continue to pile up, leading us to inadvertently create a self-perpetuating cycle of distress.

We feel anxious because we resist feeling our emotions, and we resist feeling our emotions because they make us anxious.

This avoidance comes from a fear that certain emotions will be too painful to bear. However, in sidestepping them, we unwittingly allow them to grow stronger and more persistent.

The first step in breaking this cycle is awareness. By seeing these emotions for what they are—unacknowledged fears about the future—and observing how these fears present themselves in our thoughts, behaviors, and physical sensations, we begin to strip away their power.

In a sense, we've grown complacent. That's right, we're lazy! Instead of identifying and confronting each emotion as it arises—whether it's fear, frustration, sadness, or anger—we lump them all together under the generic label of "anxiety" or "stress."

The moment we stop resisting and allow ourselves to experience these sensations fully, we begin to dissolve the dam of repressed emotional energy, freeing the river of feelings to flow naturally-relieving the pressure that feeds our anxiety.

The Unconditional Three: Finding Our Root Desires

When we PAINS, we use our emotions to amplify what is undesired, rather than to understand what is desired. What is desired is naturally the opposite of what is undesired. Appreciating this notion is powerful, as it guides you to your authentic self, aspirations, and truth.

Mattain Moment 17: Undesired vs. Desired

Let's try it—recall something you've had a strong emotion about (without overindulging in the emotion). Ask yourself, "What is undesired?" Perhaps you're not wanting to be disrespected, controlled, powerless, or hurt.

Then ask yourself, "Well, then, what is desired?" In this example, it could be to feel worthy, happy, loved, or free.

The root of all desires will fall into the category of The Unconditional Three.

Similarly, undesired experiences (like feeling disrespected, hurt, or controlled) stem from corresponding Universal Fears related to lacking these fundamental states.

At this stage, remember that it's amazing to feel. It's actually empowering to experience fear, guilt, sadness, and anger.

Not knowing exactly what you're feeling is also okay. The first step to healthier emotional processing is simply to realize what's there—to bring all your feelings into the light of your awareness, honor them, and let them be.

In the next chapter, we'll discover the Physical Body and its connection to our unacknowledged fears. We'll examine how these fears take form physically and how our bodies react to anxiety. As we continue our expanded understanding, we empower ourselves to feel, and in doing so, we continue to break down the dam of repressed emotion.

Mattain Moment 18: **Identifying Emotions**

Throughout the day, pause periodically to check in with your Emotional Body. Notice what emotions are present.

Witness each emotion without judging. For example, "I am aware of sadness," or "I am aware of anger."

Acknowledge the presence of each emotion and, through embracing it, feel any resistance to it melt away. Real pain lies in resistance to what is.

If an emotion manifests intensely through feelings, embrace it further through journaling or creative expression.

CHAPTER 6
UNDERSTANDING ANXIETY IN THE PHYSICAL BODY

Physical manifestations of anxiety might include feeling tense, stress in the shoulders and arms, a racing heart, a tight jaw, a headache, exhaustion, and pain anywhere in the body.

As we continue our investigation of unacknowledged fears, we encounter the Physical Body—a tangible canvas upon which our anxieties are etched and felt. While our mental realm may first process these fears, it's in the Physical Body that they become palpably present, evident in both sight and sensation.

Beyond the tangible—our skin, organs, bones, and blood—our Physical Body is a representation of even more than just our physiological state. It reflects our personal evolution, cultural heritage, gender identity, background, and the roles we play in society, from our educational pursuits to societal affiliations. This vessel captures the entirety of our physical self. It is directly shaped by our lived experiences and reflects the physical impact of our deep-seated convictions (rooted in the Egoic Body, shaping our Mental thoughts and influencing our Emotional responses).

Our Physical Body is the vehicle through which we interact with the world; every posture and movement mirrors our self-perception and shapes our lives.

The ultimate state of our physical being hinges on the balance between "to be" and "to do."

The state of "to be" represents pure existence, when we are present, mindful, and fully in the moment without the urge to change anything. It's the state of simply being ourselves, without judgements, masks, or pretenses.

On the other hand, "to do" signifies action and involvement in activities and goal-seeking. It's about making things happen, creating change, achieving, and actively participating in life's dance.

Both states have their significance, and our physical being thrives when we gracefully balance simply being and purposefully doing.

Alignment with The Unconditional Three

When we balance our being and doing, we embody the essence of The Unconditional Three—Worthiness, Love, and Freedom—exhibited as an alignment between our Physical, Emotional, Mental, and Egoic Bodies. In this state, we are present in each moment, free from fear or overthinking, and receptive to the fullness of our being.

Our relationship with food and drink, for example, reflects a sense of worthiness in nourishing our bodies. Healthy sleep patterns facilitate rest so we can recharge. Our ability to practice physical well-being activities becomes natural, symbolizing our freedom to move and enjoy our bodies. All of these lifestyle choices exemplify self-love and care. We find ourselves open and flexible, not just physically, but in how we perceive and interact with the world, embracing the love and connection around us.

This harmony, however, is not always maintained. When we're out of sync with The Unconditional Three, our Physical Body can succumb to a range of discomforts and illnesses. From tightness and pain to being over- or underweight, these physical manifestations reflect unacknowledged resistance residing in our other Bodies: signs we are not fully embracing our Worthiness, Love, and Freedom.

Anxiety in the Physical Body

When we're in a state of fear or anxiety, our body tends to go into survival mode—a state of heightened alertness known as the *fight, flight, or freeze* response. Our heart rate may speed up, our muscles may tense, and our breathing may become shallow.

We may notice our palms sweating, a persistent tension headache, or a knot forming in the pit of the stomach. Some may note digestive issues, like nausea or churning intestines. There could be stiffness in the neck, tightness in the back, or a tingling sensation in the extremities. Disturbed sleep patterns, marked by frequent awakenings, intense dreams, or restlessness, could also occur as manifestations of anxiety.

Mattain Moment 19: **Honoring Emotions**

Let's check in with your Physical Body right now. Where might these feelings be showing up for you?

1. **Awareness**: Take a slow breath in... and release. Gently scan your body, from the top of your head down to your toes. Do you notice any of the sensations we just discussed—tension, a racing heart, shallow breathing, a knot in your stomach, aches, tingling? Or something else entirely? Become aware of whatever physical sensations are present *without judgement.*

2. **Acknowledge & Name**: Silently acknowledge what you feel. Perhaps gently name it: "Okay, tension in my shoulders." "Hello, fluttering in my chest." "Okay, heaviness, I see you." Meet the sensation as an impartial witness.

3. **Allow**: Breathe *into* the sensation. Can you simply *allow* it to be there for this moment, without needing to fix it, change it, or push it away? Just offer it space.

These are the first steps to decoding the messages your body holds.

These reactions are not arbitrary; they're physical imprints of your fears, unacknowledged, overlooked, and looming. This state of readiness—the fight, flight, freeze response—prepares us for imminent danger. But when the danger is an unacknowledged fear rather than a physical threat, we can become stuck in survival mode, activated even when it's not necessary. Staying in this heightened state can lead to chronic pain, and even more serious health conditions such as digestive disorders, heart disease, sleep problems, and mental health disorders[6]. Aging could even be accelerated.[7]

---

[6] Mayo Clinic Staff. "Stress Management." Mayo Clinic, Mayo Foundation for Medical Education and Research, 26 Apr. 2023, www.mayoclinic.org/healthy-lifestyle/stress-management/in-depth/stress/art-20046037.

[7] Yegorov YE, Poznyak AV, Nikiforov NG, Sobenin IA, Orekhov AN. "The Link between Chronic Stress and Accelerated Aging." Biomedicines. 2020 Jul 7;8(7):198. doi: 10.3390/biomedicines8070198. PMID: 32645916; PMCID: PMC7400286.

The Body as a Messenger: Tuning into Symptoms

Physical symptoms of fear are not merely uncomfortable; they carry significant messages.

It's crucial to note that our Physical Body, just like our Emotional Body, Mental Body, or Egoic Body, isn't the culprit behind these uncomfortable sensations. Rather, it serves as a messenger, a medium through which our unacknowledged fears, limiting beliefs, and disquieting thoughts communicate with us. By tuning into these physical symptoms, we gain valuable insights into our inner self, shedding light on the fears, anxieties, and limiting viewpoints we may not even be conscious of.

Investigating the Physical Body's role in unacknowledged fears prepares us for the knowledge and practical strategies we'll uncover in the next part of this book. Remember, experiencing these physical symptoms is a natural human response to fear. Awareness of their origins is key to releasing them. Acknowledging our feelings is absolutely empowering. With this foundation, we prepare to progress onward.

Mattain Moment 20: **Body Scan Meditation**

- Adjust yourself comfortably. Bring your attention to your body, starting with your toes.

- Slowly scan your body, noticing any sensations, tension, or discomfort

- As you scan each body part, witness any expressions and simply acknowledge whatever sensations or feelings are present, without judgement.

- As you encounter areas of tension, allow their expressions. Let go of resistance and accept your state of being.

- Continue scanning your body until you reach the top of your head.

- Once you arrive at the top, allow your awareness to rest gently on your entire body for a few moments.

- Feel the wholeness of your physical being and breathe into the sense of acceptance you've cultivated.

- Take one more deep, grounding breath, and when you're ready, gently bring your focus back to the room.

By learning to listen to and honor your Physical Body, you've taken a crucial step towards wholeness. Remember, the sensations you experience are messengers guiding you towards deeper awareness and alignment across all Four Bodies. Continue practicing this acceptance, treating your body with unconditional compassion. With this foundation in understanding each of The Four Bodies, we're ready to step into their integration.

In the upcoming chapter, we'll witness the delicate dance among The Four Bodies. We'll investigate how, when in harmony and well-tended to, they lead us to a life filled with peace, joy, and freedom. However, when any Body is neglected, distress can take hold. But fear not, for with understanding comes the power to reorient, realign, and ultimately, transcend.

CHAPTER 7
INTEGRATING THE FOUR BODIES

Harmony comes from the alignment of our Egoic, Mental, Emotional, and Physical Bodies.

So far, we've examined how unacknowledged fears emerge in different facets of our being: the Egoic, Mental, Emotional, and Physical Bodies. We've found that these Bodies, crucial to our overall well-being, don't exist in isolation. They're intricately interconnected, continuously influencing and being influenced by each other.

As we've discovered, achieving balance with belief, thought, emotion, and physical sensation is a prerequisite for harmonious flourishing.

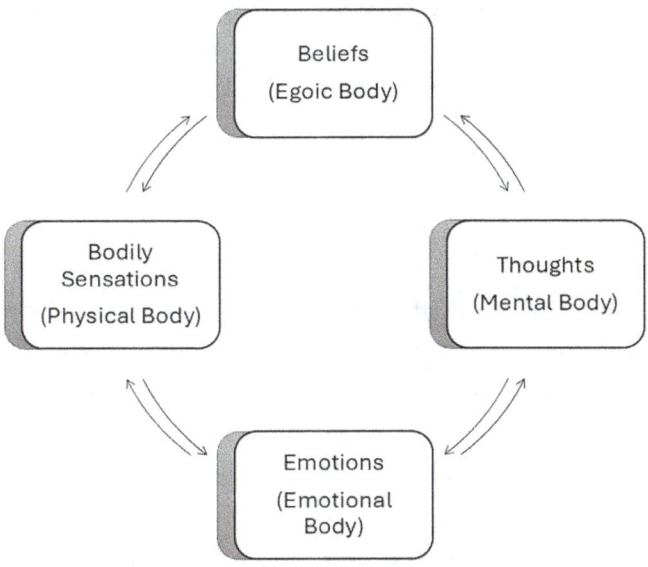

Figure 3: The Interconnected Cycle of The Four Bodies

We've come to know the interconnected cycle:
Our beliefs shape our thoughts, which in turn mold our emotions, influencing our overall state of being.

Conversely, our physical state influences our feelings, which dictate our thoughts and underlying beliefs.

We cannot merely blame a single Body for any dissonance; instead, we must grasp the interplays among them and probe the root of our manifestations.

The Roots of Self-Confidence

This intricate dance between our Four Bodies also shapes our self-perception. While we may notice self-perception through its outward expression in our Physical Body—like our posture and how we carry ourselves—this external presentation is truly a reflection of all Four Bodies. For instance, our self-confidence—how we act and carry ourselves (Physical Body)—is a derivative of our foundational self-worth (rooted in the Egoic Body), our self-image (shaped by the Mental Body), and our self-esteem (felt in the Emotional Body). All these layers are expressed through our physical being and profoundly affect our lives.

Think of it this way:

- What you believe about your value defines your self-worth (Egoic).

- How you see/think about yourself shapes your self-image (Mental).

- How you feel about yourself reveals your self-esteem (Emotional).

- Together, these perceptions inform how you act, which reflects your self-confidence (Physical).

Many of us want to be more confident, improve our self-esteem, or change our self-image. The Mattain Method teaches that true evolution in these areas requires going back to the Egoic Body—to the root cause—and exploring whether your foundational sense of self-worth is aligned with your inherent truth or if the connection feels shaky.

Anxiety and Panic

Ignoring our anxiety doesn't make it go away; it only amplifies emotions, risking a descent into panic. When panic, or "an anxiety attack," takes over, our usual line of thinking gets disrupted, overshadowed by an engulfing dread that immobilizes our mind's ability to think and process. In essence, unacknowledged fears birth anxiety, and ignored anxiety gives rise to panic.

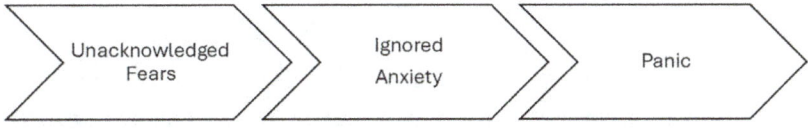

Figure 4: Escalation of Unacknowledged Fears

We interrupt the escalation of fears by seeing and addressing what lies at the root of the expressions of our Four Bodies.

Recognizing these manifestations and symptoms is crucial because it helps us see that we're not alone in our experience of anxiety, providing a sense of relief and normality. *It's important to avoid the trap of identifying with these symptoms and labels.* We're not trying to "fit" ourselves into any category; rather, we're shining a light on our fears and anxieties to better release them.

Transforming Our Relationship with Anxiety

Our goal is to evolve our relationship with anxiety. This objective requires a complete reorientation from ignoring our fears to loving our emotions, and from identifying with anxiety to genuinely comprehending and embracing the signs and symptoms of our bodies.

Recognizing and celebrating our emotions opens the door for profound self-discovery, illuminating our multifaceted existence.

Mattain Moment 21: **Aligning The Four Bodies**

Close your eyes and imagine your Four Bodies (Physical, Emotional, Mental, and Egoic) as distinct yet interconnected entities, layers, or fields of energy within and around you.

First, simply notice how they seem to interact currently. Is there a sense of overall harmony, or perhaps some friction or conflict between them? Just observe.

- Bring your focus to your Physical Body as you perceive it now. What immediate feelings or observations arise? Acknowledge whatever is present—tension, ease, frustration, acceptance. Take a breath, and on the exhale, gently release resistance to how your Physical Body is in this moment.

- Direct your awareness to your Emotional Body. How do you perceive your current emotional landscape? Notice any storylines about your feelings (e.g., "too much," "wrong," "not enough"). Breathe out, consciously releasing resistance to your emotional truth right now.

- Turn your attention to your Mental Body. What is your current relationship with your thoughts and mind? Acknowledge any assessments (e.g., "too busy," "negative," "uncontrollable"). Breathe out, releasing the need to fight or rigidly control your mind.

- Finally, connect with your Egoic Body, your core sense of self. What judgements, fears, or limiting beliefs (perhaps around Worthiness, Love, or Freedom) surface? Acknowledge these deep patterns without struggle. Breathe out, releasing resistance to your core self exactly as you are.

Having acknowledged each body and softened resistance, you've created fertile ground for harmonious alignment.

Now, in the manner best for you—whether that's visually, auditory, kinesthetically, or just "knowingly"—imagine each Body aligning with its core principles:

- Physical Body: exhibiting acceptance and ease.

- Emotional Body: radiating compassion and love.

- Mental Body: finding trust and clarity.

- Egoic Body: welcoming knowing and surrender.

As you witness this synchronization, notice how it feels in your entire being. What shifts in sensation, feeling, or thought do you notice?

Let the ego honor the mind, heart, and body.

Let the mind honor the ego, heart, and body.

Let the heart honor the ego, mind, and body.

And let the body honor the ego, mind, and heart.

Rest in this aligned state for a few moments. Give yourself a warm hug, honoring your whole self. Take one more deep, integrating breath, and when you're ready, gently bring your focus back to the room.

Now that we've dissected anxiety and how it exhibits within The Four Bodies, it's time to transcend it! The remainder of Part I will move past simply noticing anxiety to actively addressing it. In the following chapters, we'll unlock practical strategies and techniques for overcoming anxiety and cultivating a life of Worthiness, Love, and Freedom.

Ready, set, let's go!

SECTION II:
BEYOND ANXIETY

"If you think you can, you can. If you think you can't, think again."

~ Author Unknown

CHAPTER 8
SHIFTING THE NARRATIVE

Change the narrative of unacknowledged fears, and they will lose their grip on you.

We've discussed The Four Bodies—Physical, Emotional, Mental, and Egoic. We've seen how anxiety manifests uniquely within each. We've uncovered the truth about these challenging feelings: They're not monolithic "things," but a collection of unacknowledged fears expressed through our Bodies.

Now, we move from understanding to action. We transition from identifying discomfort to actively releasing it, turning unacknowledged fears into sources of strength.

Let's shift from identifying with "anxiety" to simply listening to our bodies. Many of us have allowed these types of feelings to define us and shape our self-perception.

Remember, these feelings are part of our experience, not our identity. We are not "our" anxiety. We are complex, multi-faceted beings, capable of growth, expansion, and transcendence.

Are you ready? Let's begin!

***Mattain Moment 22:* Transcending Anxiety**

Breathe in deeply, letting your breath fill your lungs, and slowly release. Become aware of this breath, of this moment, grounding yourself in the present. This simple act is a testament to your commitment and readiness to transcend anxiety.

Take a moment to pause, to move from your head to your body. Are you feeling physical tension? Where? Are emotions present? What are they: sadness, anger, fear? Are there any looping thoughts? Can you connect with any limiting beliefs?

The Mattain Method focuses on cultivating this moment-to-moment awareness and recognizing that our bodies are constantly communicating with us. It's not about eliminating difficult sensations or emotions; it's about understanding them, honoring them, and releasing the limiting beliefs that fuel them.

Transcend Anxiety Now:

- I invite you to make a conscious commitment.

- Are you willing to move beyond identifying with a label?

- Are you ready to pause and acknowledge the expressions of your Four Bodies?

- Are you ready to bring your unacknowledged fears into the light, without letting them define you?

- If your answer is yes, celebrate this moment. You've already taken a significant step towards liberation.

- You've just overcome the limitations of the label "anxiety" and opened yourself to a deeper understanding of your experience. In making that choice—to see "anxiety" as unacknowledged fear and to commit to listening to your Four Bodies—you *have*, in this crucial evolution of perspective, transcended anxiety as a limiting concept and identity.

- The sensations, emotions, thoughts, and beliefs associated with anxiety may still arise, demanding attention, but your relationship with them has changed fundamentally. *You're no longer defined by a label; you're empowered with awareness.*

In Part II, I'll provide a 5-4-3-2-1 framework to help you actively work with these expressions of your Four Bodies and align them with your inherent Worthiness, Love, and Freedom.

You have transcended anxiety.

If your answer happened to be no (to any of the above questions), that's okay, too. Simply notice *why*. What resistance are you feeling to letting go of this identity? What fears are holding you back? This insight, too, is valuable information. As you continue through this book, you'll gain tools and understanding to work with this resistance.

Return to this section of the book to develop your "muscles" of awareness. As you'll soon see, building congruence with inner truths is no different than building any of your physical muscles, like triceps, at the gym. Your understanding expands with time.

Welcome this moment of self-awareness and discovery. This milestone marks an important step forward. Celebrate and carry that momentum with you.

As we approach the conclusion of Part I, I invite you to lean into an account from Pamela. Through her courageous confrontation of unacknowledged emotions, she freed herself from mental anguish. Her achievement serves as a beacon, underscoring the power of embracing emotions for healing and growth. Remember, the strength to face our fears and honor our feelings is key to transcending anxiety. Pamela's narrative shows us what's possible.

CHAPTER 9
PAMELA'S STORY

In just moments of true understanding, lifetimes of emotional weight can be released.

Pamela, a live session participant, arrived late, her body signaling distress. She described a tightness in her chest and abdomen, a physical manifestation of the feelings consuming her. Her mind, she said, was a whirlwind of uncontrollable thoughts. She immediately expressed desperation, attributing her overwhelming feelings to her inability to quiet her mind.

Despite her regular meditation practice, which included several hours the previous night, she felt trapped and desperate. Pamela's distress was so intense, she even questioned whether people with anxiety could ever meditate effectively. Her doubt is common; many believe meditation requires a quiet mind. However, true meditation is the simple practice of awareness—even observing a busy mind is a meditative process.

The Intervention

I acknowledged Pamela's anxiety yet reframed it from a new perspective. I described it as a "lazy person's way of feeling their emotions." The underlying issue, I explained, was not acknowledging fear, which had been mislabeled as anxiety. I saw her "anxiety" as a materialization of her suppression of emotions.

I directed Pamela to move her focus from her mind (Mental Body) to her Emotional Body. I encouraged her to "surf" through her emotions and let go of internal narratives. By doing so, she could use her emotions as catalysts for freeing herself from her anxiety.

Intention and Belief: Crucial for Self-Growth

Before proceeding, I asked Pamela if she believed she could transcend her anxiety and whether she truly wanted to. I stressed the importance of intention and belief in the process of self-growth. Without the notion that change is possible and without the desire to make that change, overcoming anxiety, or any kind of inner change, is not possible. She answered yes.

At this point, pause to ask yourself: "Do I believe it's possible to overcome my anxiety? Do I genuinely want to let go of my unacknowledged fears and honor my emotions?" Take a breath and feel into your honest answers right now. Notice any resistance, any flicker of excitement or hope, any deep knowing.

Authentic belief and desire are critical for breaking free from anxiety. If you feel friction towards this step, consider it an opportunity for immediate growth and self-discovery.

You might be asking, "How do I overcome this friction?" That's a perfect and important question. This awareness of resistance—perhaps a lack of full belief or a doubt in your ability right now—is a significant insight. It demonstrates a misalignment with The Unconditional Three. For this present moment, the most powerful first step is to simply acknowledge this friction with curiosity, without judgment. Notice it. Allow it to be there. When we get to Part II, I will share the Mattain Method and 5-4-3-2-1 Framework to work through this very resistance, guiding you to understand its roots and align with your belief in yourself and your ability to achieve your desires.

The Breakthrough

When Pamela started to acknowledge her emotions rather than blame her obsessive thoughts, she had a powerful emotional reaction. She broke down in tears, marking a significant turning point. As she allowed herself to cry, she felt a knot in her chest loosen, her breath deepen, and a wave of warmth spread through her abdomen.

This physical release mirrored her emotional breakthrough. This instant unburdening of pent-up emotions symbolized Pamela's acceptance of her emotional state, a critical first step towards being in her intrinsic wholeness.

Following this breakthrough, I guided Pamela to spend the rest of the day tuning in to her body. I encouraged her to notice any physical sensations—tension, tightness, lightness, warmth—without judgement, simply observing them as they arose. I also suggested she journal about her emotions and give them a voice without analyzing them. "Let the feelings flow onto the page," I told her. "Don't try to make sense of them; just let them be expressed."

Later that evening, Pamela reported feeling a sense of release and calm she hadn't felt in years. The tightness in her chest had eased, and a sense of peace settled over her. That night, she slept more soundly than she had in a long while, evidence of the power of allowing emotions to flow.

I instructed Pamela to probe her emotions further, reiterating the importance of engaging with them rather than getting lost in the mind's narratives. By focusing on her emotions, Pamela could better manage her anxiety. I emphasized the necessity of "letting go" and "surfing through emotions" as essential strategies to mitigate unease.

Conclusion

Pamela's case illustrates the power of honoring The Four Bodies. We tend to blame our minds, but our minds are guiding us to see our emotions and our Bodies. Balancing and honoring our Four Bodies truly sets us free.

In just five minutes, Pamela underwent a major transformation that continued to deepen for years to come. By courageously facing her emotions and connecting with her body, she released a lifetime of limiting beliefs. Imagine that: a lifetime of change, beginning with a single moment of embodied acceptance. *That's* the potential that lies within these pages. And within *you*.

REFLECTIONS ON PART I: TRANSCENDING ANXIETY

The transformative power of understanding and engaging our Four Bodies sets us free. We are more than our fears and worries.

As we draw to a close in Part I, it's clear we've learned a lot together. Let's revisit the ground we've covered.

We've looked deep into the nature of anxiety, appreciating it as essentially unacknowledged fears of the future. These fears stem from our desires to align with The Unconditional Three, our lifelong pursuit of Worthiness, Love, and Freedom.

We've explored The Four Bodies—Egoic, Mental, Emotional, and Physical—which each influence our experience of anxiety. We then moved our focus to not just understanding anxiety, but actively transcending it, moving beyond the label, and adopting a fresh narrative.

Key breakthroughs derived from these chapters include:

Defining Anxiety

- Anxiety arises from unacknowledged fears about the future.

- Unacknowledged emotions can leave lasting imprints on our bodies, memories, and beliefs, shaping us far beyond any initial feelings.

- Adopting the concept that "It just is" can be extremely uplifting. Recognizing this perspective alleviates the weight of undue blame and judgements, guiding us to approach life with authentic acceptance.

Anxiety in The Four Bodies

- Anxiety is rooted in The Four Bodies, with each Body influencing our self-perception, thoughts, feelings, and physical sensations.

Anxiety in the Egoic Body

- Within the Egoic Body, we confront fears of uncertainty, feelings of inadequacy, and the challenge of finding lasting happiness.

- This realm shapes our sense of self-worth, identity, and efforts to achieve perfection.

- The foundational principles of the Egoic Body are The Unconditional Three: Worthiness, Love, and Freedom.

Anxiety in the Mental Body

- The Mental Body processes our thoughts and can intensify feelings of stress and overwhelm.

- We often blame our minds when we feel overwhelmed, yet our minds simultaneously decode information from the Physical, Emotional, and Egoic Bodies, not just the Mental.

- Once we achieve non-judgmental consciousness of the expressions of The Four Bodies, the feeling of overwhelm will subside.

Anxiety in the Emotional Body

- The Emotional Body holds on to suppressed emotions, which can contribute to anxiety.

- Avoiding or denying emotions can exacerbate distress.

- The PAINS acronym (Projecting, Amplifying, Intellectualizing, Negating, Suppressing) provides information as to common coping mechanisms.

Anxiety in the Physical Body

- Anxiety can result in physical symptoms such as tightness, pain, tension, and/or a racing heart.

- The Physical Body acts as our vehicle for interacting with the world, mirroring our self-perception and shaping our lives.

- Physical well-being and alignment involve finding a harmonious balance between "being" and "doing."

The Integration of The Four Bodies

- Unacknowledged fears are the root cause of anxiety, and suppressed anxiety turns into panic.

- Our beliefs give rise to our thoughts. These thoughts, in turn, shape our emotions, exerting a strong impact on our overall state of being. Conversely, our physical state can influence our emotions, subsequently guiding our thoughts and underlying beliefs.

- Our goal is to move from fear to freedom, from resistance to acceptance.

We achieve freedom by seeing the expressions of The Four Bodies and by addressing their root: unacknowledged fear.

Building on this foundation, I must reiterate the power of intention. Having the genuine desire to overcome anxiety is essential for self-growth; without this conviction, overcoming anxiety is an insurmountable challenge.

As we conclude Part I, we bid farewell to the terms "anxiety" and "unacknowledged fears." In Part II, we'll initiate a pivotal phase centered on self-discovery, embracing the expressions of our Four Bodies. This aim marks a new stage of our collective experience, one of elevated unity with our true selves. It's a road where we learn to take control of our narrative, rewrite our story, and reclaim our power.

Let's step into greater self-awareness, honor our fears, and even learn to love and embrace them.

Your body is speaking to you. It's time to start listening.

PART II:
FROM FEAR TO FREEDOM

When you acknowledge fear, it loses its power.

Welcome to Part II: From Fear to Freedom.

Part I: Transcending Anxiety featured the foundational "what" and the underlying "why." Now, in Part II: From Fear to Freedom, we'll venture into the practical "how" so you can achieve a greater sense of inner peace, no matter what may be going on in your life.

The next chapters will help you further understand your fears and learn to respect, honor, and maybe even love them. By discovering the value of your fears and seeing beyond them, you'll find agency, freedom, and an ability to move past the effects of fear from The Four Bodies that once limited you.

In Unveiling the Nature of Fear, which builds on Part I, we'll detail The Universal Fears and offer antidotes for each. We'll come back to the alignment of The Four Bodies. Next, Transcending Fear will present The Mattain Five-Step Process—also referred to as The Mattain Five Steps—as a comprehensive pathway from fear to freedom. Finally, we'll wrap up by putting The Mattain Five Steps into practice!

You *will* shift your Fear to Freedom.

The Essence of the Present Moment highlights the power of the now and, with The Mattain Five Steps, shows how you can remain grounded in the present.

Alchemy for Alignment provides practical techniques to achieve and maintain alignment within The Four Bodies. This section offers tools and strategies to strengthen each Body, accompanied by lifestyle and spiritual practice recommendations. We'll wrap up Part II by introducing key principles for alignment, diving into mastery, and underscoring the importance of recognizing and celebrating your personal growth.

We'll conclude with Case Studies: From Fear to Freedom, real-life examples to enrich our discussion.

Exciting discoveries await. Let's begin!

SECTION I:
UNVEILING THE NATURE OF FEAR

Your fears are not your enemies, but messengers. They carry the lessons you need to transform and transcend.

CHAPTER 10
THE UNIVERSAL FEARS

Your fears boil down to one of three: a fear of failure, a fear of being unlovable, or a fear of death. Recognizing these fears is the first step towards transcending them.

As we introduce Part II, we'll further decipher the nature of our fears. Recall that identifying these fears is a critical step towards achieving wholeness. When unchecked and unaddressed, these fears express across our Four Bodies distinctly, and the interplay among these Bodies greatly amplifies our fears.

As I highlighted in Part I, the Physical Body may respond to these fears with sensations like tension, numbness, pain, fatigue, or discomfort. The Emotional Body, burdened by suppressed emotions, may present feelings of being overwhelmed or burnt out. The Mental Body may contend with a barrage of uncontrollable and obsessive thoughts, leading to mental distress. Meanwhile, the Egoic Body, wrestling with feelings of inadequacy, isolation, and a perceived lack of control, magnifies these fears into states of feeling unworthy, disconnected, and alone, reflecting a deep misalignment with the Egoic Body's true nature of Worthiness, Love, and Freedom.

Despite their daunting nature, these manifestations are simply cries for attention. They represent the voices of our fears, eager to be seen and understood; the manifestations will persist until the fears are addressed.

As previously introduced in my philosophy, The Universal Fears connect directly with The Unconditional Three:

1. **Fear of Failure:** Linked to our primal desire for unconditional Worthiness, this fear reflects the dread of not being good enough, failure, or imperfection. We yearn for validation, measuring our worth against impossible standards of perfection. In Part I, I referred to this idea as the fear of inadequacy/unworthiness.

2. **Fear of Being Unlovable:** The fear of not finding happiness, love, or peace is connected to our longing for unconditional Love. We strive for contentment and fulfillment, fearing we may never attain the happiness we seek. In Part I, I referenced this idea as the fear of never finding love/being loved.

3. **Fear of Death:** This fear is essentially about losing control. It's tied to our longing for unconditional Freedom and can express as a desire to control our environment, future, and even the people around us in an attempt to ensure freedom and security. In essence, it's a fear of the ultimate loss of control—death. In Part I, I referred to this idea as the fear of uncertainty/loss of control.

You might observe that I've portrayed these fears slightly differently here than in Part I. That's intentional. These varied descriptions offer alternative expressions of the same underlying fears. Examining these fears from different angles enables us to relate to their many deviations. Regardless of expression, they steer us towards accordance with The Unconditional Three: Worthiness, Love, and Freedom.

Identifying which of these fears you resonate with is a critical step towards navigating them effectively.

Mattain Moment 23: **What Fear is Speaking?**

Take a breath in... and release.

1. **Tune In (Awareness):** Bring your awareness inward to your Four Bodies. Notice any subtle (or not-so-subtle!) feelings of anxiety, resistance, tension, or general unease. Where do they live in your Physical Body? What's the main emotion present? What thoughts are looping? What belief about yourself feels active in your Egoic Body? Just observe.

2. **Identify the Fear:** Gently, with curiosity, ask yourself: Which of The Universal Fears feels most connected to this feeling right now? Is it the fear of failure (Worthiness)? The fear of being unlovable (Love/happiness)? Or the fear of uncertainty/death/loss of control (Freedom)? Don't overthink it; just notice which fear resonates most closely in this moment.

3. **Acknowledge the Desire:** Now, what deep desire is this fear pointing you towards? Which of The Unconditional Three is calling out? Is it your inherent Worthiness? Your intrinsic Love? Your innate Freedom?

4. **Receive the Message:** See this fear as a messenger guiding you back to your truth. Breathe. You may wish to record any meaningful insights in your journal.

Remember, feeling fear is empowering; it's a natural human response. By observing our fears, we can navigate them with greater ease and resilience. In the subsequent chapters, we'll analyze each of The Universal Fears in depth and uncover their specific antidotes.

CHAPTER 11
THE FEAR OF FAILURE

The fear of failure is a mask hiding our fear of unworthiness. Unearth it and you will uncover your inherent self-worth.

One fear many of us grapple with is the fear of unworthiness. It's evidenced by feelings of not being good enough, striving for unreachable perfection, taking "too long" to achieve a goal, and a tendency to sabotage our own success. At its core, it's a fear that we are flawed and somehow less than we should be.

This fear of failure can also manifest in two other seemingly opposite ways. For some, it leads to avoidance—staying small, circumventing challenges, and procrastinating to minimize the risk of failing. For others, it can manifest as a fear of success itself. This may seem paradoxical, but it's rooted in the same underlying feeling of unworthiness. You may thus consider the fear of success the other side of the coin of the fear of failure. If we don't believe we deserve success, we may unconsciously sabotage our own efforts to achieve it, preventing ourselves from fully embracing our potential.

This fear of failure (or success) is usually deeply entrenched, a product of conditioning and societal expectations that have taught us to measure our worth against external standards. We were led to believe that we are not unconditionally worthy, but rather, our worthiness is contingent upon our achievements, appearance, status, and a host of other external factors.

I can certainly relate to this struggle. For many years, I considered myself a recovering perfectionist. I associated my self-worth with my output and outcomes, constantly striving to excel in everything I did. I was willing to go to great lengths to achieve perfection, sacrificing my well-being and personal desires to do so. This relentless pursuit of perfection stemmed from a deep-seated fear of failure and a view that my worthiness was dependent on doing, achieving, and external validation.

It wasn't until I embraced the essential truth that my worthiness is inherent and unconditional that I was able to break free from the grip of perfectionism. This realization led me to welcome my imperfections (as perfections), celebrate my successes, and learn from my failures *without* compromising my sense of self-worth.

This experience also reinforced the lasting impact of early conditioning and societal expectations on our perceptions of worthiness, as well as the potency of accepting our authentic selves, imperfections and all.

Mattain Moment 24: **Feeling into Worthiness**

Has anything here resonated with you? That feeling of "not good enough," the drive for perfection, or maybe even that subtle fear of success?

1. **Awareness:** Take a breath. Connect with that feeling of unworthiness or fear of failure *right now.* How does it show up in your Physical Body? Tightness? A sinking feeling? What Emotions are tangled with it? Fear? Shame? Frustration? What story is your Mental Body telling you? What's the core Egoic belief underneath? Just notice.

2. **Allowing & Compassion:** Just for this moment, can you simply *allow* that feeling to be there, without fighting or judging it? Can you offer a little compassion to the part of you that feels this way? Breathe.

3. **Acknowledge Desire & Feel Truth:** Now, acknowledge the desire underneath: the deep longing to feel worthy, capable, *enough*. Breathe into the *truth* that your worthiness isn't based on what you do or achieve; it is inherent. Can you *feel* into that truth within your heart space? Hold yourself in that space of awareness.

This awareness, this allowing, this calibration towards truth—*this* is how you reclaim your innate worth.

Many of us carry the assumption that our life is flawed or tainted. Such beliefs can arise from trauma we've endured or witnessed, like abuse, illness, neglect, or abandonment. We might internalize these events, interpreting them as personal failures that label us as "bad," "broken," or "damaged." We might consistently compare ourselves to others, wondering where we went wrong. Sentiments like "Why am I not successful/married/a homeowner/a millionaire/super fit yet, like so-and-so?" may play on a loop. This sense of being inherently "bad" due to our circumstances can intensify feelings of unworthiness.

In this cycle of self-judgement, we may also find ourselves judging and blaming others—such as our parents, caregivers, partners, family members, and friends—for our life circumstances. We might harbor a presumption that we are bad because they are/were bad, further perpetuating this cycle of criticism and blame.

However, while these experiences are undeniably painful and challenging, it's important to note that *they do not determine our worth*. Everything we go through is part of human existence and the mystery of life's unfolding. It serves our growth and expansion.

I understand this can be a challenging concept, especially when we consider profound trauma, abuse, or other deeply painful life events. My human self grapples with this notion, too. Yet my spiritual perspective allows me to surrender to the concept that even the most difficult life stories, woven into the mysterious fabric of life, can ultimately contribute to our capacity for profound strength, faith, trust, and resilience. This view doesn't negate or diminish the pain; rather, it seeks a larger context for our growth. When human comprehension reaches its limits in making sense of such life events, I invite you to lean into your own spiritual beliefs and/or deepest inner knowing for perspective.

Doing so, we see that we aren't "bad" due to our past; in fact, we aren't bad at all. We are imperfectly perfect beings moving on a path towards self-discovery and growth.

"It Just Is"

Appreciating that our parents, caregivers, family members, present and past partners, and friends all have their own unique journeys helps us release these judgements. Realizing that they, too, have always done the best they could given their circumstances and conditioning can free us from cycles of blame and self-judgement. This realization fosters compassion for ourselves and others. Recall Julia from Part I; her recount serves as an example of the eternal truth of "It just is."

As humans, we are unconditionally worthy. Our worth is not something to be earned or proven; it's intrinsic, immutable, and boundless.

We do not have to be perfect to be worthy; in fact, we do not have to be anything other than what we are.

The Antidote of Acceptance

The antidote to the fear of unworthiness is acceptance. Acceptance means affirming our *inherent worthiness* through unwavering openness to life's unfolding. It means embracing ourselves, our circumstances, and life as a whole.

While we must view our worthiness as inherently perfect, this perspective is distinct from endlessly pursuing an ideal of perfection. The goal is not to attain a superficial form of perfection, but to fully realize our absolute self-worth that stems from simply *being*.

Acceptance extends to us, our life experiences, and our entire journey. This acceptance goes beyond intellectualization; rather, it's about true feeling and embodiment. We find profound freedom when we realize "It just is."

Many people believe they can simply recite affirmations like "I am worthy," "I am free," or "I am love," and expect a quick turnaround in their lives. They may create vision boards and repeat these statements daily, hoping for things to improve. However, if deep down they don't truly *know, believe, and feel* they are worthy, love/loved/lovable, or free, these affirmations might create resistance instead of fostering the desired outcome. Overcoming anxiety isn't just about changing your thoughts; it's about transforming your *entire being*.

Harmonizing your beliefs (Egoic Body), cultivating trust (Mental Body), embracing your emotions (Emotional Body), and grounding yourself in the present (Physical Body), is the pathway that allows an expansive sense of freedom to blossom. The Mattain Method, which I'll detail in the following section, goes beyond surface-level affirmations. A five-step process that actively engages your Physical, Emotional, Mental, and Egoic Bodies, this technique allows you to transform your beliefs at the foundational level. This holistic approach is what sets The Mattain Method apart.

Thinking is not enough. The key is to harmonize The Four Bodies.

By recognizing our unquestionable worthiness through absolute acceptance, we can release the fears that have held us back. Through this radical acknowledgement, we live authentically and applaud our true selves.

Now that we've addressed the fear of failure, let's adventure into another universal fear—one that touches the core of our Emotional Body—the fear of not being loved.

CHAPTER 12
THE FEAR OF NOT BEING LOVED

We search for love externally, forgetting that the truest source of love lies within us.

The fear of not being loved, of being unlovable, or of never finding happiness, love, or peace is a deeply human fear many of us navigate. It's connected to our innate longing for unconditional happiness, a state of contentment and fulfillment that seems elusive. We strive towards this aspiration, haunted by the fear that we may never attain the level of happiness we seek.

One of my core beliefs, which I invite you to consider adopting, is that at our essence, **we *are* love and light.**

This conviction is not only empowering, but also serves as a beacon, guiding us towards self-discovery, truth, and authenticity. We're all navigating a course towards unconditional love, happiness, joy, and peace—one that guides us to our authentic selves.

As discussed in Part I, societal conditioning and life's circumstances distort our conceptions of love, happiness, joy, and peace. We've come to see these feelings as external, conditional states to be achieved, rather than internal, unconditional qualities to be uncovered. The word "love" in particular has been laden with so many conditional meanings which fail to convey its true essence. Hence, I choose to use a combination of words—love, happiness, joy, peace—to signify the essence of unconditional Love.

The distortions I speak of are reflected in many aspects of our lives, from our search for romantic relationships to our longing for a happy family, and even in the pain of separation or divorce. We seek love and happiness outside ourselves, not realizing that these are states of being we source from *within*.

When we don't acknowledge our fears—such as being unlovable, never finding love, or ending up alone—these feelings might be mistaken for what we previously labeled "anxiety." Yet, by pinpointing these fears, we begin to reframe our perspective.

Instead of drowning in overwhelming feelings, realizations emerge:

- "Oh, this isn't anxiety; these are fears waiting to be uncovered."

- "Ah, that made me feel really bad. Oh, I feel rejected. What does that mean? Oh, I know…"

- "Wow, digging deeper, I feel unlovable beneath that rejection."

- "I've never recognized this fear before. It's intriguing. I wonder where I acquired this misbelief?"

- "What is my ultimate truth?"

Engaging in this exploration can be metamorphic.

Mattain Moment 25: **Feeling into Love**

Did you relate to that inner dialogue? The realization that beneath the surface might be a fear of being unlovable, indicating a deep longing for happiness or inner peace? Let's unpack this idea right now.

1. **Awareness:** Pause. Take a breath. Tune into your Four Bodies. Where does that fear of being unlovable, or the intense longing for love and happiness, show up? Is there an ache or emptiness in your Physical Body? A familiar sadness, anxiety, or loneliness in your Emotional Body? What stories does your Mental Body spin about finding love or being accepted? What core belief about your lovability is in your Egoic Body? Just notice as an impartial observer.

2. **Acknowledge the Desire:** Gently acknowledge the deep desire underneath this fear—the desire for unconditional love, connection, happiness, peace. Recognize this longing as a pull towards your own essence, because love is what you are.

3. **Connect Within:** Now, bring your attention to your heart. Can you place a hand there? Even amidst the fear and longing, can you sense a tiny spark of warmth? A flicker of compassion for yourself for feeling this way? Breathe into that inner space. This is where the love that you seek truly resides.

This awareness, this acknowledgement of desire, this turning inward—this is how we begin to dissolve the fear of being unlovable and remember the love we already *are*.

So, what's the antidote to these unconscious beliefs and fears? Let's find out!

The Antidote of Compassion

To counter the fear of being unlovable, we turn to compassion. This antidote finds its roots in our true nature. At our very core, we are beings of love and light. This concept is a universal truth that we overlook amidst the noise and chaos of the external world. Lost in a sea of fears, doubts, and insecurities, we lose sight of the love within us—the love we are made of.

The fear of being unlovable stems from an intense longing for love. We are unconsciously driven by the question: "How can I be loved more fully?" Interestingly, the answer is embedded within the desire itself.

What does this mean? It means that the very longing for love is a powerful inner compass, guiding us back to the truth that love isn't something we lack and must find "out there." Rather, the desire itself arises because, at our core, we are love. The intensity of the desire simply points to where we have become disconnected from this inherent truth. The path to feeling "loved more fully," therefore, involves turning inward to uncover, allow, and embody the unconditional love that is our essence.

So, how do we cultivate this love? Through both passive and active expressions of compassion. Though compassion and love have their own nuances, they are intertwined, forming the foundation of human connection, understanding, and empathy. They often intersect: Love can envelop compassion, and compassionate acts can magnify feelings of love. If you're looking to nurture and radiate your inner love, compassion is your pivotal instrument. To actively cultivate this compassion, particularly if it feels unnatural at first, try this: in moments of difficulty, consciously pause and ask what a deeply loving friend or wise guardian would say to your current self. Then, offer those same words of kindness and understanding directly to yourself.

We seek love from others, forgetting that we are its very source. We look for love in external validation and approval, oblivious to the abundance of love within us. The fear of being unlovable stems from this forgetfulness and disconnection from our true nature.

To truly welcome this reality is to tap into our inherent source of love, happiness, joy, and peace. When we realize that we are not lacking in love, but rather that we *are* the embodiment of love, a potent awakening occurs.

We no longer seek love. We embody the love that we are.

We no longer pursue happiness. We radiate happiness.

These truths are key to overcoming the fear of being unlovable. Embrace loving compassion, live it, and let it guide you inward towards your radiantly authentic self.

In the next chapter, we'll cover one of my favorites that always comes up during my coaching and livestreams: the fear of death—and its antidote.

CHAPTER 13
THE FEAR OF DEATH

Change is life's only constant. Surrender to this truth, and you'll align with life's innate freedom.

Among the most intense fears we grapple with are the fear of freedom and its counterpart, the fear of control. These fears are strongly rooted in our primal discomfort with life's uncertainties. We yearn for predictability, for a future we can forecast and shape. But life, in its infinite complexity, refuses to be boxed into our predictions. Uncertainty and lack of control amplify our fears, leading to what we previously referred to as "anxiety."

This fear of uncertainty, this discomfort with the unknown, extends beyond our immediate circumstances. It's essentially a fear of life, a fear of death, a fear of freedom, a fear of being alone, a fear of both control and losing control. It's our struggle to comprehend our human experience within the vastness of the universe, coupled with the fear of recognizing our lack of control over life's most significant events.

The realization that our coming and going is not in our hands, but rather in the hands of a power unknown to us, can be a source of existential fear.

The Certainty of Life and Death

In life, there are only two certainties: life itself, and death. Although Benjamin Franklin famously quipped that the only certainties are death and taxes, many millions of people don't pay taxes, so some might say they're better at dodging taxes than death! And yet, the very certainty of death often fuels our deepest fears and anxieties.

We have no control over when life is given, nor taken away. These events are perhaps the greatest mysteries we face. If you believe in God, surrender to His/Her/Their plan. If you believe in The Universe, trust in its flow. Whatever your views—whether rooted in spiritual faith, a deep connection to humanity and nature, or a commitment to personal principles and rational thought—lean into them wholeheartedly to find peace in the face of life's uncertainties.

Realizing and releasing our illusion of control over when life begins and ends can free us from the fear of death, allowing us to move through life with greater ease.

Mattain Moment 26: **Feeling into Control & Freedom**

Let's feel into that freedom right now.

1. **Awareness**: Take a breath. Tune into your Four Bodies. Where does the *need* to control, or the *fear* of uncertainty/loss of control/death, materialize within you?

    °   *Physical Body:* Notice any tension, clenching, restlessness, or holding patterns.

    °   *Emotional Body:* What feelings are present? Anxiety? Fear? Frustration? A subtle unease?

    °   *Mental Body:* Are there looping "what if" thoughts? Perhaps constant planning or worrying? Self-judgmental "whys" or "if onlys?"

    °   *Egoic Body:* What underlying beliefs are active? "I must be in charge," "The unknown is dangerous," or "I'm not safe?"

2. *Acknowledge the Desire:* Gently acknowledge the deep desire beneath the fear: the longing for peace, ease, trust, genuine *freedom*. Recognize this pull towards your inherent state, one of The Unconditional Three.

3. *Allow Uncertainty:* Now, just for this moment, can you simply *allow* the feeling of uncertainty? Can you breathe *with* the reality that you don't control everything, without needing to immediately fix it or find an answer? Just *be* with the not-knowing, even if it feels uncomfortable. Allow the resistance to be there, too.

4. *Flow with Freedom:* As you stop fighting for control, notice any subtle softening, any space opening up within you. True freedom is found in accepting life's flow, not controlling it. Feel into that truth. Allow.

This fear of death is often unrecognized, although prevalent in society. Many people say they are "control freaks," identify as "anal," or simply state they "don't like to lose control." These expressions are just different ways of voicing the underlying, unacknowledged fear of death, reflecting the fact that life in and of itself cannot be controlled.

The Only Constant in Life Is Change

Life's only certainty (aside from its beginning and end) is its constant evolution. Recognizing this truth and surrendering to the changeability of life are crucial to calibrating to absolute freedom.

When you find yourself fearing life's uncertainty, remember that it's an oxymoron. *Change is not only expected; it's a guarantee.* Embracing this constant is the first step to harmonizing with freedom and transcending the fears of control, lack of control, death, and uncertainty.

Mattain Moment 27: **Feeling into Change & Flow**

Let's feel how that truth—*change is the only constant*—lands in your body right now.

1. **Awareness of Resistance**: Take a deep breath. Tune into your Four Bodies. As you consider the idea that everything is always changing, where does resistance show up?

    ° *Physical Body:* Any tightness, bracing, holding?

    ° *Emotional Body:* Any fear, anxiety, unease?

    ° *Mental Body:* Thoughts like "I don't like change," "This is scary," or "I need a plan?"

    ° *Egoic Body:* A clinging to the familiar? A belief that change is bad?

2. **Awareness of Flow**: Now, can you sense anywhere in your being, even a tiny spark, that feels okay with change, maybe even curious or excited about it? Where might a feeling of flow, ease, adventure, or freedom surface when you imagine simply allowing change?

3. **Allowing**: Notice both the resistance and the capacity for flow. Can you hold space for both feelings without judging them? Breathe into that space.

This paradigm shift is the beginning of harmonizing with life's constant evolution and finding freedom within it.

Interestingly, this fear of uncertainty/death/control can actualize in two distinct ways:

- Some of us respond by exerting excessive control over our lives, leading to a constant state of tension as we attempt to suppress the natural ebb and flow of existence. This typically futile striving can take the form of obsessive tendencies, perfectionism, or an overwhelming need to micromanage every detail, establishing a rigid and inflexible approach to life.

- Others might choose a route of apparent relinquishment of control or responsibility. They might turn to substances like drugs or alcohol, use food for comfort, gamble, and/or partake in adrenaline-fueled activities that create an illusion of control while masking a deeper fear of losing control. Indeed, this core fear of powerlessness often propels the search for control in many forms—from these temporary illusions to more direct efforts to manage oneself, others, or life's unpredictable nature.

However, whether we're tightening our grip or seemingly letting go, we're not truly addressing the root fear. Neither path—over-controlling or a misperception of letting go by under-controlling—is conducive to true peace and liberation. Both are merely strategies to avoid facing our underlying fears.

The Antidote of Trust

The antidote I propose to this fear is "trust." Trust in oneself, in life, in the unfolding of life, and in a greater power.

Whether you associate this trust with a divine entity—be it God, The Universe, your inner being, higher self, or whatever you call the enigma of the unknown—the essence remains the same. This trust serves as an affirmation that *there is more to life than our human experience.* It's a surrender to life's flow and an acceptance of the ever-unfolding present.

This trust is not only about the broader universe; it is intensely personal. It's about self-trust. It's about trusting our ability to negotiate life's twists and turns, finding confidence in our resilience and adaptability. It's about perceiving that while we cannot control external circumstances, we can always choose our responses.

By recognizing our fear of control and acknowledging our discomfort with uncertainty, we start to release these suppressed fears. Trust serves as our guiding light, illuminating the road to liberation. Trusting in The Universe, in life, in God, in our inner being, in a higher power—these are all expressions of the same fundamental trust. Trust that life is unfolding as it should, trust in the rhythm and flow of existence, and trust in your ability to move through life.

As we continue, we'll unveil practical strategies and steps to better acknowledge and release these fears while we move towards liberation.

CHAPTER 14
ACT FOR ALIGNMENT OF THE FOUR BODIES

In the flow of life, ACT—Acceptance, Compassion, Trust—is our rhythm, guiding us to harmonious alignment.

As we examine our fears further, an essential concept has emerged. For each of The Universal Fears, we have an antidote. Combined, these antidotes form a powerful framework, which we shall refer to as "The Antidote." This trio—Acceptance, Compassion, and Trust (ACT)—serves as not only a direct response to our fears, but also a compass guiding our alignment.

In our prior discussions, "alignment" emerged as a central theme. Remember from Part I that alignment entails synchronizing The Four Bodies with the foundational truths of The Unconditional Three as well as with each other. By seeing our fears as guides rather than barriers, we move closer to this alignment.

To further appreciate the role of ACT, let's break it down:

Acceptance: Acceptance extends to all aspects of our being. It's about embracing our physical selves, our emotional experiences, our mental processes, and our egoic conceptions, appreciating them as integral facets of our wholeness and the unfolding of life. It's about welcoming the full spectrum of human experiences, without judgement or the need to categorize them as good or bad, success or failure. It's about determining that every moment, whether joyful or painful, expected or unexpected, contributes to our growth and evolution.

Acceptance ultimately guides us to an authentic sense of Worthiness, Love, and Freedom, enabling us to cherish our true selves without criticism. It's about realizing we are enough, just as we are, and our value is not contingent on our achievements or our ability to meet external expectations or certain timeframes. Acceptance is the gateway to self-worth.

Compassion: Compassion is an emotional radiance that comprises actions, feelings, thoughts, and beliefs directed towards ourselves, life, and the human journey. Compassion provides the bridge that helps us traverse feelings of not finding love, feeling unlovable, and unhappiness. Compassion is the conduit to love.

Trust: Our progression through life generates fears of the unknown, the uncontrollable, and ultimately, death. Cultivating trust involves tapping into deeper life meanings, placing faith in ourselves, our life's course, and the vast mysteries and greater meaning and purpose of life. Trust is the channel to expansive freedom.

When ACT is embedded within our Four Bodies, it guides us towards congruence with our innate Worthiness, Love, and Freedom.

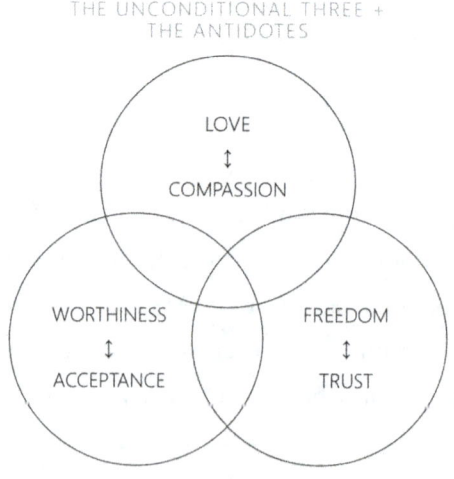

Figure 5: The Unconditional Three and ACT as The Antidote

Through this lens:

- **Acceptance** is primarily an expression of the *Physical Body* that guides us towards ease in our physical self and life course.

- **Compassion** radiates from our *Emotional Body,* signifying our capacities for care and kindness.

- **Trust** emanates from our *Mental Body,* reflecting our fortitude and unwavering faith amidst life's uncertainties.

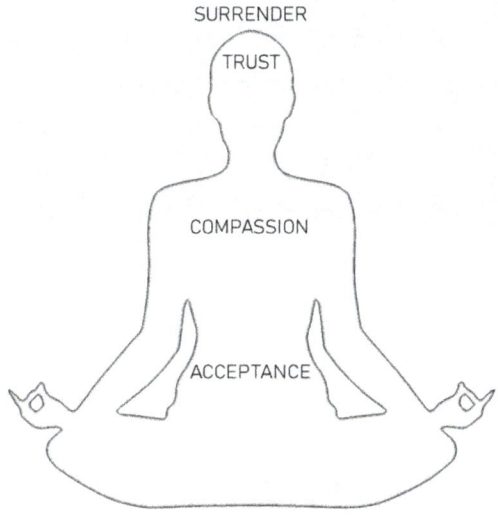

Figure 6: ACT as an Expression of The Four Bodies

ACT may also manifest through any of The Four Bodies. Consider Compassion: There are acts of compassion (Physical), sentiments of compassion (Emotional), thoughts of compassion (Mental), and a foundational belief in the beauty and goodness of humanity (Egoic). However, the core elements of ACT predominantly resonate as Acceptance in the Physical Body, Compassion in the Emotional Body, and Trust in the Mental Body (we'll look more deeply at the Egoic Body's role in a moment).

I've emphasized this idea before, and it bears repeating: Don't just intellectualize these concepts. Trying to mentally force these truths or grasp them through sheer will, rather than allowing an integrated knowing, can easily devolve into "efforting." This state of strenuous pushing paradoxically blocks the very embodiment and alignment we seek. Instead, I invite you to genuinely know, trust, feel, and be these principles.

Revisiting core Mattain tenets captures this essence. The sentiments "It just is" and "It's hard, until it's not" act as touchstones for authentic *Acceptance*. The idea that "Our conditioners were conditioned, and their conditioners were conditioned" calls us to relish in genuine *Compassion*. Contemplations such as "The only constant in life is change" and "In life, there are only two certainties: life itself, and death" are designed to fortify your *trust* in the natural flow of life.

Can you see the tremendous role ACT plays in orienting The Four Bodies? With ACT, we've harmonized three of The Four Bodies.

Mattain Moment 28: Embodying ACT

Let's *feel* that harmony right now. Take a deep breath in... and release.

1. **Feel Acceptance (Physical Body):** Bring awareness to your Physical Body. Can you soften any tension you're holding? Intentionally invite a feeling of acceptance for your body, exactly as it is in this moment. Feel the grounding, the ease that acceptance brings.

2. **Feel Compassion (Emotional Body):** Now, bring attention to your heart space, your Emotional Body. Cultivate a feeling of warmth and kindness towards yourself. Offer compassion for yourself, for your journey, and for all your feelings. Allow that compassionate energy to fill you.

3. **Feel Trust (Mental Body):** Gently let your awareness settle upon your Mental Body. Let go of any need to know or figure things out right now. Invite a sense of trust—trust in yourself, trust in this process, trust in life's unfolding. Feel the calm that arises when you trust.

4. **Integrate:** Notice how these three qualities—Acceptance, Compassion, Trust—feel *together* within your being. Sense the alignment, the quiet strength, the connection to your inherent Worthiness, Love, and Freedom. This feeling *is* coming home to yourself.

What happens when the Egoic Body fully aligns with our harmonized other three Bodies? Resistance dissolves. You stand infinite, free, and deeply centered.

Are you intrigued? Move on to the next chapter!

CHAPTER 15
SURRENDER, THE PINNACLE
OF ALIGNMENT

Surrender is the art of fully allowing life's flow, a profound alignment born from Acceptance, Compassion, and Trust.

Surrender, the natural culmination of deeply embedding Acceptance, Compassion, and Trust within us, represents a state of completely permitting life's unraveling. This state, free from resistance, signifies the ultimate harmonization of The Four Bodies. While resistance obstructs and creates friction, surrender eases and allows. When we surrender, we are resistance-free; when we are resistance-free, we surrender. This term, symbolic of the highest state of being, is the focal point of this chapter.

While I haven't extensively touched on "surrender" in the earlier sections of this book, its significance emerges undeniably now. *Surrender stands as the pivotal fifth step of The Mattain Five-Step Process,* which you'll soon become acquainted with.

While the term "surrender" might evoke images of defeat or giving up, it actually represents embracing and trusting life fully. In essence, to surrender is to master life.

By cultivating ACT—Acceptance, Compassion, and Trust—we facilitate synchrony within our Four Bodies.

We've come to understand:

- Anxiety is unacknowledged fears about the future.

- It is exhibited through The Four Bodies.

- Its primary forms are the fears of failure, being unlovable, and death.

- These fears relate to The Unconditional Three: Worthiness, Love, and Freedom.

Our lifelong pursuit is alignment with The Unconditional Three.

The antidote to these fears is ACT—Acceptance, Compassion, and Trust—which also leads the way to wholeness.

The road towards embodying ACT culminates in Surrender, referred to as "ACTS" in Mattain-Speak.

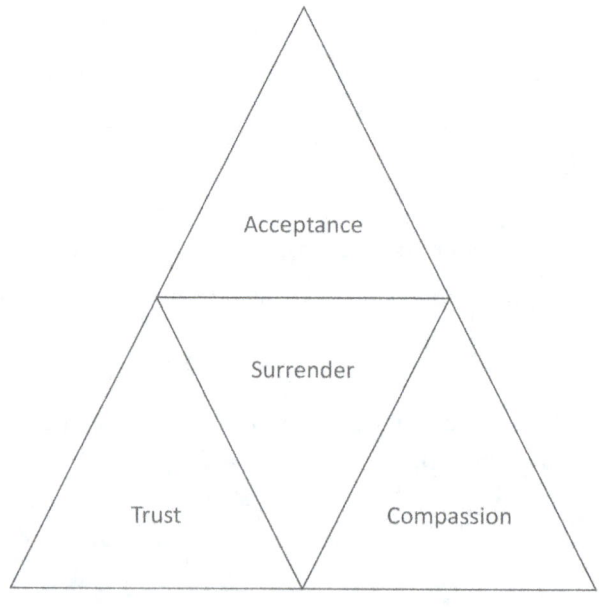

Figure 7: ACTS

We've come to the point where Acceptance, Compassion, Trust, and Surrender harmoniously orient The Four Bodies, guiding us to a state of allowing, flow, and beauty. This alignment not only enriches our lives but also accentuates the elegance of our multifaceted existence.

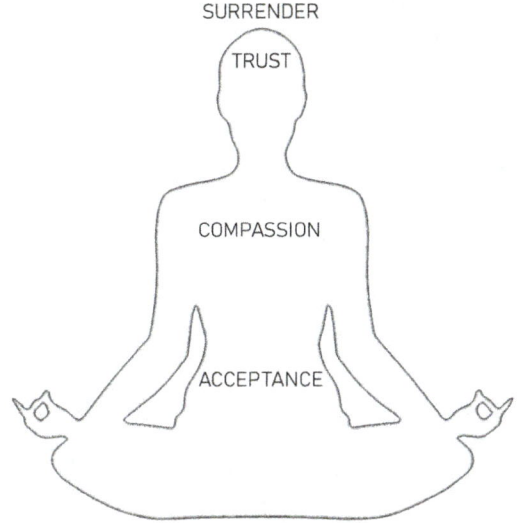

Figure 8: The Four Bodies in Harmony

At this juncture, more questions arise:

- What is the path to overcoming our deepest fears?

- How do we cultivate qualities such as Acceptance, Compassion, and Trust within ourselves?

- How can we then align with Surrender?

In the upcoming section, Transcending Fears, I'll introduce The Mattain Five-Step Process designed to guide you past your fears, towards alignment, and to the discovery of your true self through surrender.

SECTION II:
TRANSCENDING FEAR

Transcending fear is not about eliminating it altogether but about understanding its message and transforming its energy.

CHAPTER 16
THE MATTAIN FIVE-STEP PROCESS

Turn fear into freedom in five simple steps with The Mattain Method.

Our progress to this point has prepared us for an essential step: learning *how* to objectively see and release our fears. Up to now, we've identified symptoms of what we previously termed "anxiety" across our Four Bodies. We've unearthed hidden fears and learned to become aware of them. Now, we're ready to challenge our interpretations of these fears from subjective experiences into objective observations.

In this section, we'll walk through The Mattain Five-Step Process carefully crafted to guide us in seeing our fears objectively. This system can be used to transform resistance of any form in any of The Four Bodies, whether it manifests as:

- Physical discomfort like chronic pain or persistent tension

- Emotional turmoil such as fear, anxiety, guilt, or shame

- Mental patterns like looping thoughts or self-critical judgments

- Egoic constrictions rooted in limiting beliefs about worth, happiness, freedom, or capabilities

Guilt, Shame, and other Resistance

A quick word on guilt and shame: While anxiety is unacknowledged fear projected onto the future, guilt and shame function as judgements of the past.

Although their time focus differs, these experiences all represent forms of resistance blocking our authentic truth.

Guilt and shame manifest as judgments of something not being good enough or us not being good enough. The antidote is the same—recognize that you are doing the best you can with your circumstances and always have done the best you could given wherever you were at a specific time.

Here's the good news: The Mattain Method's 5-4-3-2-1 Framework applies universally; it provides a reliable path to process these judgements, whether past- or future-oriented, ultimately returning your awareness to the power and peace of the present. The Mattain Method applies to *any* energy—anxiety, fear, guilt, shame, and anything else—preventing you from your innate Worthiness, Love, and Freedom.

Consistent with the theme of this book, we'll focus primarily on fears; we'll confront them directly and set ourselves free from "anxiety."

The Mattain Five-Step process helps us move past judging our fears as "bad" or "good," encouraging us to instead explore the information they hold. As demonstrated by Julia's story in Part I, the greater value is arriving at "It just is." Our fears are simply here, directing us inward and pointing us to greater desires connected to our ongoing pursuit of The Unconditional Three.

Here is an overview of The Mattain Five-Step Process:

Step 1: Awareness

This step involves becoming cognizant of our fears across all Four Bodies: Physical, Emotional, Mental, and Egoic. Through Awareness, we see, observe, and discern fear for what it truly is: an external indicator pointing us inward towards what is desired.

Step 2: Acknowledgement

This stage represents acknowledging what we truly desire (and don't desire). Once we're aware of what is undesired, which we uncover in Step 1, we can easily identify what is desired. This step is so powerful because it orients us internally towards our true essence.

Step Three: Appreciation

After Acknowledging our fears, we move towards appreciating that they are guiding us to our deeper desires. We come to see these fears as gifts that help us grow. Feeling this appreciation authentically is key. As we covered in Part I, doing so is a sign of growing alignment within The Four Bodies.

Step Four: Allowing

After Appreciating our fears (Step 3), this pivotal step is about unconsciously releasing resistance to whatever arises in our Four Bodies. We practice simply allowing these physical sensations, emotions, thoughts, and beliefs to be present without fighting them, recognizing that suffering stems from resistance, not the expressions themselves. This non-resistance creates space for "a-ha" moments, authentic release, and deeper alignment.

Step 5: Surrender

Surrender, the fifth and final step, is less an action and more a state we arrive at. It is the ultimate alignment of The Four Bodies, characterized by unconditional acceptance of all that is. In this state, we deeply surrender to our experiences, to life, and to The Universe, embodying a place where ACT—Acceptance, Compassion, and Trust—are our natural way of being.

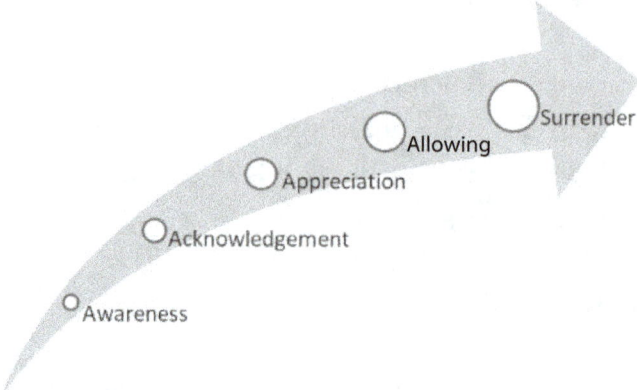

Figure 9: The Mattain Five-Step Process

Did you notice that I described "Surrender" as a state of unconditional acceptance? Much like the foundational practices of Awareness, Acknowledgment, Appreciation, and Allowing, Surrender isn't about "doing" in an effortful, external sense. Instead, it is the culmination of these ways of being—a state of embodied, unconditional acceptance achieved through mastery of ACT. Steps 1-4 lay the essential groundwork of awareness and internal alignment, enabling us to fully embody the ultimate state of Surrender. Perhaps the most profound application for Surrender involves life's ultimate certainty: death. This topic requires immense sensitivity. Surrender here is not about suppressing sadness or denying loss but about releasing resistance to this inevitable reality.

I sometimes witness individuals nearing the end of life, with no other options, continuing to fight desperately. This resistance creates immense suffering. Conversely, I also see individuals who arrive at a place of peace and acceptance. They have surrendered, releasing the fight against the inevitable. Their Four Bodies radiate a sense of inner calm rooted in Acceptance, Compassion, and Trust.

Similarly, for those left behind, grief is unavoidable. Yet there's a difference between grieving and denying the reality of loss. Surrender, for the bereaved, involves fully allowing the deep pain of grief while simultaneously accepting reality. It means cultivating trust, finding compassion for ourselves and others, and grieving fully without getting stuck in resistance to what is.

The Mattain Five-Step Process serves as a guide to identifying and remodeling fears. In subsequent chapters, we'll dissect each step in depth. We'll end by walking through the five steps together and applying them to your fears (and more).

These five steps give you all the tools you need to understand and shape not only your fears, but all resistance you may navigate in your Four Bodies: fear, anxiety, guilt, shame, and anything else that may be blocking you from achieving The Unconditional Three. As we progress together, we're moving beyond fear towards the Worthiness, Love, and Freedom that lie within us. You will recalibrate to the resonance of your authentic self.

CHAPTER 17
STEP ONE: AWARENESS

Awareness is the first step on the path to transformation. Embrace it, for it is the key that unlocks the door to freedom.

As we've been practicing together throughout this book, developing awareness is fundamental. Fittingly, The Mattain Five-Step Process begins with Awareness. This step involves cultivating awareness of your fears and perceiving how they show up within your Four Bodies. Awareness involves observing your physical sensations, feelings, thoughts, and viewpoints without judgement.

It's important to not become overwhelmed by limiting beliefs, thoughts, emotions, or physical sensations. Instead, choose to view them as symptoms or signals pointing to your desires. By recognizing that these resistant feelings stem from important root causes, you take the first step in transformation.

I encourage my clients to visualize themselves as journalists, explorers, detectives, investigators, or third-person narrators observing their Four Bodies. This approach helps move away from excessive self-indulgence and judgement and promotes a more objective identification of sensations—a higher, less emotionally charged perspective.

As part of fostering Awareness, we metaphorically "surf" our Four Bodies. This practice entails observing the rise and fall of physical sensations, emotions, limiting thoughts, and misbeliefs, comparable to riding ocean waves. You are not submerged in the waves—you are moving with their flow.

Here's another powerful way to connect with your Four Bodies: "taste" them. Just as you savor the complex notes in a delicious meal, you can learn to "taste"—to deeply sense and discern the unique energetic quality of—your physical sensations (like tightness or ease), emotions (like sadness or joy), thoughts (like confusion or clarity), and beliefs (like "I am not enough" or "I am worthy"). This practice will allow you to experience everything that's happening inside with a new level of nuanced awareness.

Mattain Moment 29: **Tasting**

Let's "taste" our inner world. Bring something to mind—a feeling, a situation, anything coming to your awareness right now. It may be a thought, pattern, or sensation you perceive as "negative" or "positive," or you may not have a connotation for it either way.

Now, instead of analyzing it, try to sense its unique energetic "flavor" or quality. Can you discern this subtle essence? For example, what's the energetic "flavor" of sadness? Of anger? Of fear? Of joy? Tuning into experiences this way—metaphorically "tasting" their physical manifestations and expressions—is an effective way to feel objectively, bypassing the analytical mind and connecting directly with felt senses in your body.

Another aspect of this method is "naming," where we might utilize labels or identities to better understand our physical sensations, emotions, thoughts, and beliefs. For instance, my editor playfully offered examples from her own life, calling her meticulous editor self "Ms. Persnickety Pants" and her affectionate side "Madame le Cuddlebear." Some labels I've noticed or used for myself include "recovering perfectionist," "idea-generator," or "eternal optimizer." Recognizing the labels we assign can be insightful; notice how they might reveal attachments to certain ways of being, perhaps illustrating a need to prove "worthiness" through perfection or constant optimization, for example. While these labels can be valuable for comprehension and validation, it's essential to use them consciously, rather than letting them define us. Our primary objective is to broaden our grasp of these sensations without becoming attached to any particular identity.

While surfing through our bodies, we may notice sensations within the Physical Body. Investigating these physical sensations with curiosity and intrigue can be quite impactful. Don't try to figure out why they are there, or "fix" them. Just stay open to what your body may be trying to communicate, simply observing, not identifying directly with any tightness, numbness, or specific sensations.

These physical sensations offer valuable glimpses into our emotional states. Permitting ourselves to feel these sensations without passing judgement is essential. Adopt an inquisitive approach to observing the expressions of your Emotional Body. Welcome fully the texture of any emotion that arises and be curious about the emotion itself and its associated sensations.

For example, when I notice tension in my jaw, a racing mind, and tight shoulders, instead of getting caught up in negative thoughts or blame, I simply observe these sensations with curiosity. I acknowledge the discomfort, explore the emotions that might be connected to it, and find ways to cultivate comfort and acceptance, enabling me to interpret the experience without friction and create space for healing and growth.

The Mental Body is where stories and narratives take shape. Intentionally distinguishing your narratives from your beliefs, emotions, and sense of self is crucial. Narratives amplify fears, leading to a spiral of anxious thoughts, which can disconnect you from awareness of the expressions within The Four Bodies and take you into your head. By purposefully refraining from identifying with these narratives, you move closer to aligning The Four Bodies.

Mattain Moment 30: **Tuning In**

Before we continue, take a moment to simply *tune in*. Notice any physical sensations. Notice any emotions present. Notice the flow of your thoughts. Notice any underlying beliefs. Just *be* with what is.

To deepen our exploration of these manifestations and their interconnectedness, I will now introduce one of my foundational concepts: Deconstructing the Key Lime Pie.

Deconstructing the Key Lime Pie

I liken the act of distinguishing the expressions, signs, and symptoms of our Four Bodies to breaking down the layers of a pie. Just as a Key Lime Pie is layered with graham crackers, lime filling, whipped cream, and a cherry on top, recognizing the expressions of The Four Bodies helps us fully grasp their unique characteristics. This perception opens the door for us to dissect these expressions and uncover our core truths.

When you encounter resistance within your Four Bodies, your goal is to break down the layers of the Physical, Emotional, Mental, and Egoic Bodies.

You can use prompts such as:

- What is my body trying to convey?

- What message might my physical pain be sending?

- What information is held in my emotions or desires?

- What do the stories in my mind signify?

- What beliefs, limiting or otherwise, are emerging?

As discussed in Part I, all resistance stems from what is undesired. These undesired feelings relate to the fear of failure, fear of not being lovable, fear of death, or their variations. Continue to permit your awareness to move within your Four Bodies until you pinpoint these fears. Acknowledge them. Respect them. Cherish them. Love them.

Mattain Moment 31: **Deconstructing the Key Lime Pie**

Let's put Deconstructing the Key Lime Pie into practice. Take a deep breath and tune into your inner landscape. You can choose to explore how you're feeling right now, or you may deliberately invite into your consciousness a specific event, situation, or encounter (perceived "positive" or "negative") that you've experienced. Whichever you choose, the intention is awareness; try not to overindulge in the stories, emotions, and sensations. Simply observe them as we move through each layer.

---

1. **Physical**: Taste the Graham Crackers. Scan your body. Do you feel a particular sensation? Notice its quality—tightness, warmth, buzzing? Can you taste its unique flavor, just as it is?

2. **Emotional**: Try the filling. What emotion, whether tangy like lime or sweet like meringue, is present, even subtly? Can you surf its wave, observing its rise and fall without getting carried away?

3. **Mental**: Enjoy the whipped cream. What thought just passed through? Can you simply witness it (the story, worry, memory, planning, evaluation, etc.) without attachment?

4. **Egoic**: Indulge in the cherry on top. Is there an overarching belief or self-perception present? ("I am not good enough," "It's not my fault," "I'll never get this," or "Life is hard."). Can you just observe it without judging?

This exercise embodies Awareness—allowing the expressions of your different layers with radical acceptance.

Now, let's consider a real-life example. I recently worked with a client, Joanne, who came to me feeling overwhelmed and anxious. She had just lost her job and, tragically, had to put her beloved dog down. When I asked Joanne how she was feeling, she said, "I just want to feel good."

I laughed—I tend to do that during moments of high resistance, maybe my subconscious way of releasing it—and said, "How are you going to feel good when you've just lost your job and your dog? Have you considered connecting with your emotions to see how they actually feel?"

After a little laugh, she paused, and said, "I feel alone and lost. I'll never get better."

"Those are powerful words," I replied, "and they contain a mix of things. 'Alone' and 'lost' point to feelings, but 'I'll never get better'—that's a thought, tangled with limiting beliefs from your Mental and Egoic Bodies. Let's set the thought aside for now. How do you truly feel, deep inside?"

Joanne took a moment, tuned in, and then said, "Oh! I feel so sad. My heart hurts." And she broke down crying.

I smiled and replied, "Amazing! Yes, it would be incredibly painful to go through the loss and uncertainty you've described. Two losses back-to-back. By allowing these feelings, you're releasing the dam of emotions you've been holding back—what you were calling 'anxiety'—and letting them move through you."

Instead of trying to immediately force normalcy or "feel better," Joanne later shared that she gave herself permission to simply be with the sadness when she was home. She described consciously holding herself with compassion, like a loving friend would, allowing the waves of grief and loss to wash over her without judging or needing to rush the process. This allowing, this acceptance of her emotional reality was the true beginning of Joanne's recalibration towards inner peace.

As you see with Joanne, real breakthroughs happen when we move beyond mental stories and connect directly with the sensations and emotions in our Four Bodies. Let's establish that connection now.

Mattain Moment 32: **Embracing Your Emotions**

Take what you learned from that example and apply it to yourself. Simply *notice*. Don't try to change anything. Just allow yourself to be *aware* of what's happening within you.

1. **Find the Resistance:** Bring to mind a current situation or feeling that's causing you discomfort—what you might typically label as anxiety, stress, or overwhelm.

2. **Taste Your Physical Body:** Activate your sense of taste. Scan your *Physical Body*. Where do you feel the resistance? What is its unique "flavor" or energetic signature? Does it feel bitter, salty, tight, heavy, burning, or numb? Explore with openness.

3. **Taste Your Emotional Body:** What emotions are present? Sadness? Anger? Fear? Frustration? *Taste* them. What are the flavors of these emotions? Bitter? Sour? Tangy? Dull?

4. **Taste Your Mental Body:** What thoughts are swirling? Are they judgmental? Fearful? Anxious? *Taste* the qualities of these thoughts.

5. **Taste your Egoic Body:** What beliefs about yourself and the world are influencing your experience?

6. **Surf the Sensations:** Now, imagine yourself *surfing* these sensations, emotions, thoughts, and beliefs. You're not *in* the wave, drowning in it; you're riding it, observing it, allowing it to move with you.

7. **Name and Release:** As you taste and surf, give each sensation, emotion, thought, and belief a name. This simple act of naming helps to create distance and dis-identification. As you name each, imagine its intensity diminishing and flowing out of your body with every exhale.

Can you see the power of tasting, surfing, naming, and releasing your resistance? Power lies in becoming intimately familiar with the language of your Four Bodies, so you can respond with awareness and compassion, rather than reacting from a place of fear and resistance.

Awareness is the first step in releasing resistance and moving towards wholeness.

Cultivating the ability to move into an open state of Awareness when resistance is high is not always easy. We're conditioned to react, blame, judge, and be comfortable as a "victim." Recall this principle: "It's hard, until it's not." Just like building a muscle, this process requires consistent focus.

The more you commit, the more adept you'll become at surfing your Four Bodies and moving beyond your fears. I frequently underscore this principle as it naturally nurtures a genuine sense of self-compassion and acceptance.

In summary, Step 1: Awareness serves as a potent guide that enables us to immerse ourselves in our encounters with fear and transform them expertly. Through the recognition and comprehension of our fears, we grow past them, ultimately moving towards a life of Worthiness, Love, and Freedom.

With this foundation of Awareness established, we're ready to move on to Step 2 of The Mattain Five-Step Process: Acknowledgement.

CHAPTER 18
STEP TWO: ACKNOWLEDGEMENT

Shift from unwanted to wanted, from fear to freedom, from challenge to opportunity. Acknowledgement empowers you to transform your experiences.

We now turn to Step 2: Acknowledgment, where empowerment begins. We begin the process of redirecting our attention from what is undesired to what is desired. We begin to see our fears not as obstacles to be overcome, but as signposts directing us towards our true desires.

With Step 1: Awareness, we tuned into ourselves, taking note of pronounced sensations. We applied the construct of Deconstructing the Key Lime Pie to identify expressions of The Four Bodies: physical pain, resistant emotions, looping thoughts, misbeliefs. We exposed strong expressions of what is undesired, what is unwanted. Within this awareness of the unwanted lies the seed of what is wanted or truly desired. **From unwanted to wanted, or from undesired to desired**—this is the "gift of fear."

This reframe of perspective is immensely powerful. When we truly see, feel, believe, and know that *the obstacles in our lives are pathways to our dreams and aspirations,* our entire journeys become empowering. The experiences we encounter are no longer roadblocks; they're stepping stones guiding us inward to our deepest desires.

The Unconditional Three play a crucial role here. As we learned in Part 1, *everything external leads us internally.* The Universal Fears—fear of failure, fear of being unlovable, and fear of death (or some derivative thereof)—guide us from external calibration to internal calibration.

Layer	Body	Undesired (Resistant State)	Desired (Aligned State)
Cherry on Top	Egoic Body	Limiting beliefs (unworthiness, lack of control), fear of failure/success, feeling "not good enough," "not lovable," or "not free"	Worthiness, Love, Freedom, "I AM"
Whipped Cream	Mental Body	Looping thoughts, negative self-talk, worry, over-analysis, criticism, stories, "what ifs"	Open-mindedness, clarity, focus, trust, positive self-talk
Lime Filling	Emotional Body	Fear, anger, sadness, grief, shame, guilt, resentment, anxiety, loneliness	Peace, acceptance, joy, compassion, love, contentment, emotional balance
Graham Cracker Crust	Physical Body	Tension, pain, discomfort, illness, fatigue, numbness	Ease, flow, vitality, health, presence, grounded-ness

Figure 10: Deconstructing the Key Lime Pie

This synchrony is directed towards The Unconditional Three. Thus, we come to see, "Oh, this isn't about my fears; It's about my desires for Worthiness, Love, and Freedom."

Let's consider some examples.

- If you feel out of control, controlled by others, or overly exerting control (carrying too much responsibility or micromanaging), then you may desire Freedom.

- If you feel like a failure, not good enough, or driven to perfection, then you may desire Worthiness.

- If you feel sad, angry, alone, or unloved, then you may desire Love, happiness, joy, and peace.

We can also explore this idea from an external perspective.

- If you long for more money, better health, or opportunities to travel, then you may internally desire Freedom.

- If you want a successful career, healthy body, or recognition, then you may internally desire Worthiness.

- If you'd like to manifest fulfilling relationships, enriching friendships, or memorable experiences, then you may internally desire Love, happiness, joy, and peace.

For all these examples, any desire could point to one, two, or even all of The Unconditional Three. Through "surfing" your expressions and Deconstructing the Key Lime Pie (as described in Step 1), such actualizations can be made.

***Mattain Moment 33:* From Undesired to Desired**

Let's put these concepts into practice.

1. **Identify the Unwanted:** Bring to mind a current challenge or discomfort—something you'd typically label as "bad," "struggle," or "anxiety" (or a manifestation of it).

2. **Deconstruct the Key Lime Pie:**

    °   *Physical Body:* What physical sensations are present? *Taste* them.

    °   *Emotional Body:* What emotions are you feeling? *Taste* them.

    °   *Mental Body:* What thoughts are looping? *Taste* them.

    °   *Egoic Body:* What underlying beliefs are fueling these experiences? *Taste* them.

3. **Surf the Sensations:** Now, imagine yourself *surfing* these sensations, emotions, thoughts, and beliefs. You're not *in* the wave; you're riding it.

4. **Name the Fear:** What is the *core fear* underlying these expressions (e.g., fear of failure, fear of not being loved, fear of uncertainty/loss of control)? Don't judge it; simply name it.

5. **Flip the Script:** Now, examine: What is the opposite of this fear? What is the desired state I'm truly seeking?

    ° If you feel like a failure (or are driven by perfectionism): You desire *Worthiness*.

    ° If you feel sad, lonely, or angry: You desire *Love*.

    ° If you feel out of control (or overly controlled or controlling): You desire *Freedom*.

This reframe in perspective—from focusing on the unwanted to recognizing the desired—is immensely powerful. This outlook encapsulates the essence of the "It just is" philosophy: acknowledging what is (the fear, the discomfort) without judging it, and using that awareness as a springboard to move towards what you truly want (Worthiness, Love, and Freedom).

Our fears are arrows guiding us towards our desires.

Acknowledging these unwanted feelings or states is not about dwelling on or amplifying them. Rather, it's about seeing them as indicators of our deeper desires. They serve as reminders of our constant pursuit of The Unconditional Three, illuminating the direction to our authentic self.

By recognizing what we don't want, we gain clarity on what we *do* want. This Acknowledgement is a powerful conduit for transformation. It moves our focus from the unwanted to the wanted, from challenge to opportunity, from fear to freedom.

In the next section, we'll learn how to leverage this Acknowledgement to appreciate our fears as guides towards our greatest desires. By embracing the unwanted, we clear the way for what is wanted, elevating every life occurrence into the actualization of our dreams.

Can you see how I am fulfilling my promise of helping you move from fear to freedom? Exciting, yes? Let's continue!

CHAPTER 19
STEP THREE: APPRECIATION

Appreciation is the bridge between fear and love. It transforms our perspective, turning obstacles into opportunities.

Appreciation, the third step of The Mattain Five-Step Process, is pivotal in reshaping our fears. Having surfed our Four Bodies to understand the expressions of the undesired and flipped the narrative to pinpoint what is truly desired, we're now poised for Step 3: Appreciation. Recall from Part I that this appreciation shouldn't merely be intellectualized; it must emanate from a place of authenticity. Authentic appreciation is genuinely seen, felt, believed, and trusted.

As we move through this step, we evolve from feeling victimized to empowered. We transition from taking life personally to owning our experiences, viewing them as opportunities for growth. Such an awakening nurtures an enriching sense of appreciation and ease that infuses our entire essence, symbolizing the "It just is" aspect of life.

But how do we foster this Appreciation? Here's where things become even more intriguing. A quick recap:

- **Step 1:** We identified our fears, stemming from The Universal Fears, as they manifest in the unfolding of life.

- **Step 2:** We discerned that these fears are guiding us inward, towards The Unconditional Three. This epiphany prompts us to cherish our life experiences, synchronize with our deepest desires, and understand our authentic selves.

- **Step 3:** By applying one or more of the three Antidotes—Acceptance, Compassion, and Trust (ACT)—we transmute fear:

  ° Fear of failure directs us to Acceptance.

  ° Fear of not being loved directs us to Compassion.

  ° Fear of death directs us to Trust.

By embracing these principles, we tap into the empowering nature of life. We foster a radical Acceptance of all that is, grounded in our Physical Body; cultivate Compassion through the lens of our Emotional Body; and establish Trust, anchored in the Mental Body. These ACT sentiments are the coordinated expressions of the Egoic Body in harmony with our Physical, Emotional, and Mental Bodies. This harmony is the essence of alignment, the very embodiment of Surrender—a complete allowing of life to flow without resistance.

Navigating Steps 1, 2, and 3 might require several rounds, especially when addressing deep-rooted conditioning. Yet with sustained focus, commitment, and intention, arriving at authentic appreciation becomes intuitive.

Crucially, this appreciation doesn't come from intellectualizing our external circumstances or forcing ourselves to "find the good" in difficult situations. It arises from an internal calibration—connecting with our inherent wholeness and trusting the larger mystery of life, even during challenges.

Example: Finding Appreciation Amidst Loss

Let's revisit Joanne, the client I mentioned earlier who was feeling overwhelmed after losing her job and her beloved dog. Initially, she was stuck in grief, sadness (Emotional Body), had a physical ache in her heart (Physical Body), noted looping thoughts of loss and hopelessness ("I'll never get better"—Mental

Body), and expressed an underlying belief of loss of love and connection ("I'm alone and lost"—Egoic Body).

After Awareness (Step 1) and Acknowledging the desire beneath the fear (Step 2)—perhaps success (Worthiness), connection (Love), and security (Freedom)—we moved to Appreciation (Step 3), which catalyzes embodying ACT through feeling, not intellectualizing.

- **Acceptance:** Acknowledging the reality: "Okay, this loss happened. It hurts intensely. It just is right now." Accepting the fear of the unknown future.

- **Compassion:** Offering self-compassion: "It's understandable to feel this sad and scared. This is incredibly difficult." Replacing self-judgement with kindness.

- **Trust:** Cultivating trust, even amidst uncertainty: "I may not know how right now, but I trust I can do this. I trust in my own strength."

Through the lens of ACT, an opening developed. While sadness was still present, Joanne started to feel appreciation for the deep love she shared with her dog, for the happy memories. She appreciated the enduring spiritual connection, recognizing death not as an end, but as part of life's greater mystery. She began to appreciate her own strength in facing job loss, the skills she possessed, and the support system she had, recognizing that her worthiness was internal and unchanged by her employment status. The intense charge of her initial emotions began to lessen as appreciation grew—not by denying the pain, but by holding it alongside a recognition of the gifts within the experience. That's *authentic* appreciation.

Mattain Moment 34: **Appreciation Through ACT**

Bring to mind a fear or challenge you identified in Step 1: Appreciation.

1. **Acknowledge Desire** (Recap of Step 2): Which of The Unconditional Three (Worthiness, Love, or Freedom) does this fear point you towards?

2. **Apply ACT:**

   ° Can you find Acceptance for the situation, just as it is right now? Breathe into it.

   ° Can you offer yourself Compassion for the feelings this situation brings up? Place a hand on your heart.

   ° Can you cultivate Trust in yourself, in the process, or in life's unfolding? Feel that sense of grounding.

3. **Notice Appreciation:** As you hold Acceptance, Compassion, and Trust, notice if any genuine appreciation arises. Appreciation for your strength? For a lesson learned? For a connection made? For the simple act of breathing through it? Don't force it; just observe.

4. **Taste and Surf:** Taste the feeling of appreciation, however small. Surf this feeling, allowing it to expand.

Continue this practice, allowing appreciation to bridge the gap between fear and love.

True appreciation is a gateway to revolutionary power. It unites us with the infinite potential within us and helps us become powerful navigators of life. This step is a celebration of growth, resilience, and the beauty of self-discovery. Step 3 teaches us to love our journey, every step of the way.

Enjoy this process, for here you cultivate authentic appreciation for yourself and the unique unfolding of your life. With the foundation of Awareness, Acknowledgement, and Appreciation firmly established, let's move forward to Allowing.

CHAPTER 20
STEP FOUR: ALLOWING

Releasing fear is like exhaling after a long-held breath; it's a return to a natural, effortless state of being.

Allowing, the fourth step of The Mattain Five-Step Process, marks the point where we begin to feel lighter. This step is much like reaching the peak of a mountain after a strenuous climb. The challenge decreases, and the perspective changes. True Allowing is not an act of control from the ego, as in thinking, "I am choosing to Allow this." It arises from a place of pure flow and non-resistance.

I used to call this step "Releasing" or "Letting Go," but "Allowing" more accurately captures its essence. This step isn't about forcing release; it's about creating the space for it to happen *naturally*. It's about ceasing to resist the physical sensations, emotions, thoughts, and notions that arise. By simply *allowing* these expressions of energy to be present, without judgement or interference, they dissipate naturally.

This isn't an act of *doing*, but an act of *undoing*—of letting go of the grip, the control, the resistance. With an openness to trust and a willingness to feel, this path is surprisingly "easy."

Through authentically experiencing Appreciation for ourselves and our life experiences in Step 3, we transformed our energy. With this newfound perspective, we're ready to allow the fears we initially connected with in Step 1 to flow and shift, naturally and with ease and grace.

Example: Allowing Grief to Flow

Grief is a powerful space in which Allowing is crucial. We resist, feeling we "should be strong" or "get over it," trapping heavy emotions in the body. My "Mourning Meditation" on Insight Timer guides listeners through this very process. Listeners often share how impactful the simple progression to *Allowing* is.

The primary aim is to honor the grieving process—to feel the sadness, the anger, the emptiness, whatever arises—without getting lost in limiting stories or beliefs. My meditation guides listeners to feel without evaluating or needing to fix anything.

By creating this non-resistant space and stopping the fight against grief's natural flow, listeners report a significant release. Tears flow freely after being held back; deep sighs escape unconsciously; physical tension held for weeks, months, or even years begins to soften.

Allowing isn't an act of forcing grief away; it's simply letting its energy move through you. This non-resistance, this simple act of *giving permission for the emotion to be,* is the essence of Allowing. In fact, Allowing is not just applicable to emotions, but also to physical manifestations, mental thoughts, and egoic misbeliefs. This release is the natural exhale after holding your breath for too long, leading to an unexpected yet welcome sense of lightness and peace emerging alongside any sadness or other emotion.

Mattain Moment 35: **Allowing**

Allowing can be both conscious and unconscious. Here are a few conscious approaches:

- **Visualize**: You may visualize your resistance dispelling from your body and returning to the light, perhaps as smoke drifting away.

- **Breathe with Intention:** Take a deep breath in, acknowledging the resistance. With the exhale, consciously set an intention to let go, imagining the resistance leaving with your breath.

- **Move Your Body:** If walking is your preference, as it often is for me, imagine each step relinquishing resistance back to The Universe or down to Mother Earth. Dancing, shaking, or any form of intuitive movement can also facilitate release.

Any thought, intuition, or belief that facilitates release is encouraging. Have fun exploring the approach or mix of techniques that resonates with you.

I'm always amazed when I see someone I'm coaching instinctively take a deep breath, signaling an unconscious release of resistance. When they indulge in a deep breath in, followed by a heavy release, they're typically not even aware of this natural reflex. This release can also manifest as a strong outpouring of emotion, such as tears or shaking. I encourage you to free your body to let go in whatever way feels right, in tandem with your conscious intention to release.

To release fears is to truly let go, akin to shaking off a heavy backpack after a long trek or shrugging off an itchy sweater. The moment we decide to let go, we feel an immediate sense of relief and lightness.

If you still feel any heaviness after this step, that's perfectly okay. You may need to cycle through Steps 1-4 again. At times, you may uncover a resistant emotion that was hidden beneath the original one. This finding could require a bit more tolerance, Acceptance, Compassion, and/or Trust as you peel back the layers.

Each time you revisit these steps, the process becomes more fluid, reminiscent of the muscle analogy I frequently mention. Just as one new to exercise might initially find bicep curls challenging, those new to The Four Bodies and Steps 1-4 may initially find the process "hard." Yet with consistent intention and repetition, "It's hard, until it's not."

Relish every phase of this evolution. Each round not only strengthens and hones your "muscles," but also fosters growth and inner strength. Keep going. The next step is Surrender!

CHAPTER 21
STEP FIVE: SURRENDER

To surrender is to accept all of life's unfolding, recognizing that every obstacle is a gift when approached with Awareness, Acknowledgement, Appreciation, and Allowing.

Surrender, the fifth and final step of The Mattain Five-Step Process, is not so much a step as a *state*. Surrender is the ultimate state of alignment of The Four Bodies, of unconditional Acceptance, Compassion, and Trust (ACT), of all that is. Surrender is the state of embracing life fully, the mastery of life, the mastery of Steps 1-4, and the *recognition that every experience is a gift*.

Now, I deeply recognize that seeing profound trauma—such as abuse, violence, severe illness, or devastating loss—as holding any kind of "gift" can feel difficult, inappropriate, or even impossible from our human perspective. And that feeling is completely valid. Acceptance does not mean condoning harm or pretending pain isn't real. For many who have navigated unspeakable events, the path to alignment and Surrender does not involve finding a "gift" in the trauma itself. Instead, it entails acknowledging the full reality of the pain with immense self-compassion, and perhaps, over time, recognizing the incredible strength, resilience, wisdom, or capacity for love we discover within ourselves because we navigated that experience. The "gift," in this context, might be the discovery of our own unbreakable spirit or a deeper connection to truth. This capacity for reframing and finding strength, even in darkness, is also a "muscle" we build. When our human understanding struggles, I invite you to lean into your spiritual beliefs and/or deepest knowing, trusting the possibility of finding meaning or expansion even when the path is unclear. This deep trust, even without full understanding, is fundamental to Surrender.

To surrender is to accept life's flow. To be in a perpetual state of Allowing. To yield to The Universe, the experiences we encounter, and the broader mysteries and meanings of life. Within this realm, we find peace and honor all emotions, letting them serve as our guides.

With this enlightened awareness, we find that no event is innately "bad" or "good." "It just is." This perspective redefines our engagement with life, catalyzing us to experience it fully, through all its highs and lows.

A Personal Example: From Frustration to Surrender

Let me share a personal example of moving through The Five Steps to arrive at a state of Surrender. I recall an occurrence while driving in the car with one of my children where intense frustration and anger surfaced within me.

I think it's beneficial to clarify—for my own empowerment—that my child didn't do anything to me, nor did they make me feel that way; to believe otherwise would be to give away my power. Rather, the exchange merely sparked a pre-existing "vibrational misbelief" or imprint I carried. This internal activation was what ultimately led me to question my core sense of worthiness and, as a result, feel so intensely misaligned.

The specific details of what happened aren't the focus here. What mattered was the intensity of my internal response across all Four Bodies—the physical sensations, the rush of emotions, the reactive thoughts, the underlying beliefs that were activated. Such a strong reaction showed me I was out of alignment.

Whether the specific incident that induced this strong reaction felt significant or insignificant, "justified" or "unjustified," is irrelevant to the process. Our Four Bodies respond based on a myriad of factors, including deep conditioning. The important point isn't analyzing or judging our Bodies' reactions; it's learning how to listen to these internal signals to use them as guides back into alignment.

This is the process I used—and that you can use, too—to return to center, regardless of what initially knocked me off balance.

Step 1: Awareness. In that moment, I instinctively tried to observe, to taste the heat, the tension, the sheer passion rising in my body. But I quickly recognized, nope, neither the time nor the place. I needed to be present. So, I promised myself, "Okay, Manal, we're revisiting this later." That evening, I settled in and invited the memory back—not just the story, but the felt senses. I re-experienced the heat, the tightness (Physical Body), the frustration and anger (Emotional Body), the "How could they?!" thoughts (Mental Body).

Step 2: Acknowledgement. As I surfed the intensity, I asked, "What's under this?" Ah, the familiar sting: "I'm not good enough," "I'm taken for granted," "Nothing I do is ever enough" (Egoic Body). The core fear was unworthiness. And the flip side, the desire? To simply know, deep down, that I was worthy, unconditionally.

Step 3: Appreciation. Here's the shift: a soft smile. I recognized this pattern. It wasn't about my child; it was my old narrative. It was The Universe offering another chance for me to really get that *my worth isn't dependent on anything outside of me.* Suddenly, I felt appreciation—for my willingness to see, for the pattern itself showing me where to grow, for The Universe providing the lesson. It wasn't personal; "It just is (was)." That's Appreciation: finding the gift, the opportunity for growth, even in a difficult moment. Applying ACT, I accepted the situation, felt compassion for myself and my child, and trusted the process.

Step 4: Allowing. And then, whoosh—a deep sigh I didn't even consciously take. The heat dissipated, the tension released, and the intensity softened. I felt instantly lighter. That's Allowing—the natural consequence of genuine appreciation. Resistance dissolves when it's met with Acceptance, Compassion, and Trust.

Step 5: Surrender. What followed was delicious. That feeling of surrender, my favorite state. Acceptance, allowing, ease, flow. Pure presence. Just *being*.

Achieving Surrender represents the culmination of The Mattain Five-Step Process—a moment where passive reactions to life give way to active creation. This state leads us to a life of Freedom, embedded in Love and Worthiness.

The Mattain Five-Step Process is a comprehensive approach. Steps 1-4 are active undertakings that integrate the principles detailed in Part 1, while Step 5 represents a state of mastery.

Ready to apply it? Let's put The Mattain Five Steps into action to shape your fears into freedom.

CHAPTER 22
THE MATTAIN METHOD:
AS EASY AS 5-4-3-2-1

The Mattain Method: your simple roadmap from fear back to your authentic self.

We've learned a powerful method for transforming our relationship with fear, which I refer to as The 5-4-3-2-1 Framework. We've discovered how to work through *Five* Steps: Awareness, Acknowledgement, Appreciation, Allowing, and Surrender. We've listened to the wisdom of our *Four* Bodies: Physical, Emotional, Mental, and Egoic. We've uncovered *Three* Unconditional Desires: Worthiness, Love, and Freedom, that lie beneath all our fears and aspirations. We've recognized *Two* States: moving from undesired (resistance) to desired (allowing). And we've unveiled the power of "It just is"—the liberating potential of radical acceptance, leading us to *One* Truth: "I AM," beyond all labels, conditions, and limitations.

Now, let's put it all together. The Mattain Method is a simple yet powerful framework for moving from resistance to allowing, from fear to freedom.

This, in essence, is the 5-4-3-2-1 of The Mattain Method: a roadmap from fear to freedom, from fragmentation to wholeness. It's a straightforward structure for substantial transformation. By applying these principles, you can overcome life's challenges with greater ease, connect with your inner wisdom, and live from a place of authentic power. Ready to jump in?

CHAPTER 23
APPLYING THE MATTAIN METHOD

Fear is not an enemy; it's a compass pointing us to areas where we need to grow.

Now that we've learned The Mattain Five-Step Process, we will transcend fear. We've arrived at the point we've all been waiting for! To recap:

Step 1: Awareness is the initial step in transcending fear, involving tuning into our Four Bodies as third-person observers to understand their expressions of what is undesired (our fears).

Step 2: Acknowledgement is where we identify our hidden desires that have been suppressed yet are now illuminated by our fears.

Step 3: Appreciation entails seeing our fears as gateways to our aspirations, cultivating an authentic expression of the idea that nothing is personal, that life isn't happening to you; it's happening *for* you.

Step 4: Allowing is where we detach naturally and deliberately from resistance to fears. We do this both unconsciously—yawning, sighing, crying—or consciously—letting a deep breath out, shaking, or imagining a physical release.

Step 5: Surrender is a state of mastery of Steps 1 through 4 where we fully embrace a state of ACTS: Acceptance, Compassion, Trust, and Surrender.

Now, we'll apply The Mattain Five-Step Process together, and transmute fear into Worthiness, Love, and Freedom. You may find it helpful to have a journal nearby to note your experiences as we proceed.

Approach this practice with self-compassion; if any part is overwhelming, feel free to pause and return when you're ready. Do this in one session or break it down—listen to your body (actually, listen to all Four of them!). This is a liberating transition, and you are fully capable of navigating it. Here we go!

Mattain Moment 36: **Transcending Fear**

To begin, pause and take a moment to breathe in deeply, letting your breath fill your lungs, and slowly release.

Become aware of this breath, of this moment, grounding yourself in the present. Notice the feeling of air entering and leaving your nostrils, the rise and fall of your chest, the gentle expansion and contraction of your abdomen. Now, take two more deep, conscious breaths, savoring each inhale and exhale.

Awareness: Gently guide your attention inward, noticing the subtle sensations within your Physical, Emotional, Mental, and Egoic Bodies as you invite the feeling of fear from a place of curiosity.

To do this, you might bring to mind a past experience, a specific fear you hold, a challenging memory, a persistent "anxiety," a particular person, or a significant event. You could also gently invite a misbelief, such as the feeling of being out of control or unlovable. For some, the feeling of fear may arise easily with just the intention to observe it.

Welcome the fear as a feeling to understand with the intent to observe, honor, and respect it.

As you draw in another deep breath, revel in the empowerment arising from this heightened awareness of your Four Bodies and their varied expressions.

Now, let's Deconstruct the Key Lime Pie, approaching each layer with curiosity:

Physical Body (Graham Cracker Crust): What are the physical manifestations and sensations of fear? Where do they resonate within your body?

Emotional Body (Lime Filling): Dive deep with curiosity. What emotions are you feeling? What emerges? Can you discern different shades or nuances in your fears?

Mental Body (Whipped Cream): What thoughts, stories, or memories surface? What are the earliest memories you have of these sentiments? Let them emerge without judgement. Stay open and curious.

Egoic Body (Cherry on Top): What misbeliefs or limiting beliefs do you notice as you navigate your Four Bodies? How might these beliefs relate to The Unconditional Three?

As you surf your Four Bodies, ask yourself, "What is this resistance telling me? What is undesired?"

Take your time. Immerse yourself in the experience, and let it unfold naturally. Enjoy.

Acknowledgement: By acknowledging your fears, you can redirect your perspective from what is undesired to desired.

Now that you're aware of the specific fear or expression of the "undesired" (from Step 1), this step leads us to acknowledge what is desired. Recognize that within every fear or expression of unwanted lies the clear reflection of what is wanted.

Own that your fears guide you to your desires. Let your mind sift through these fears to expose their corresponding desires.

Let your awareness rest on any specific undesired feeling or situation identified earlier. Ask yourself directly: "If this is what I don't want, then what is the opposite I truly do want?"

Perhaps the immediate answers that arise are aspirations related to your external world: nurturing relationships, optimal health, a fulfilling career, financial success, creative expression, etc. Take note of these external, surface, or situational desires.

Then, the crucial step: *Go deeper to find the core motivation.* Distill these surface desires down to their root internal drivers. Ask yourself: "What core feeling am I truly seeking through achieving this external goal (like the relationship, health, or success)?"

Invariably, you will find these powerful external desires connect back to the most fundamental human yearnings—The Unconditional Three— the need to feel Worthiness, to connect with your unconditional Love, and/or to live in absolute Freedom. Recognize these as the internal desires fueling the external ones.

Breathe deeply, savoring the heightened self-awareness and clarity this acknowledgment offers.

Appreciation: Cultivating authentic appreciation through ACT—Acceptance, Compassion, and Trust—leads you to transform your fears into The Unconditional Three: Worthiness, Love, and Freedom.

Apply ACT whenever and wherever needed as you surf through your Four Bodies. Dive into the sensations of Acceptance, Compassion, and Trust, feeling each in its entirety as it resonates within. Lean into your wholeness and the deeper meaning of life.

By mindfully engaging with your Four Bodies and truly honoring their presence, you allow their uplifting energy to surface.

Pause to admire this milestone. Embrace this moment. Celebrate your growth. Savor the warmth of your introspection and follow the rhythm of your breath.

Allowing: You are ready for the unconscious and conscious act of releasing your fears, the act of letting go. As you do, you'll find yourself feeling lighter, more liberated, and more closely aligned with your authentic essence.

Now, you stand poised to release the resistance of the Physical, Mental, Emotional, and Egoic Bodies.

Simply be present with whatever sensations, feelings, thoughts, or misbeliefs have arisen from your awareness in the previous steps. Without any need to alter, fix, or judge them, just allow these expressions of your Four Bodies to be, noticing them with gentle, open awareness. This is the heart of Allowing: simply being with what is, right now.

Inhale deeply. On the exhale, envision this resistant energy leaving you, flowing towards a luminous beacon, whether it be the core of The Universe, a radiant light, or The Divine.

Root yourself in Acceptance of who you are, Compassion for your path, and Trust in the unfolding of life.

Breathe deeply once more, holding it for a moment. And as you exhale, release any lingering resistance, fully surrendering to the intricate beauty and mystery of the human experience.

Once again, rest here for a moment. Simply sit with the presence of your Four Bodies, allowing whatever is now to simply be.

If you don't immediately feel a sense of lightness or if a trace of heaviness persists, that's perfectly okay. You can revisit steps 1-4, moving at a pace that feels right for you. Immerse yourself in the sensations of your body, avoid over-analyzing, ride the waves of your emotions, and place unwavering trust in yourself and the course you're on.

Surrender: The final state of Surrender is a realization; it is a full embrace of life, a robust acceptance of each experience and the gifts it brings.

Take a moment and breathe deeply. Let yourself be enveloped by a sanctuary of Acceptance, Compassion, and Trust. This feeling is the essence of the present moment, fully inhabited. It's in this space that we can truly yield to life's flow, trusting the greater mysteries without needing to control or understand everything.

Applaud the Worthiness, Love, and Freedom that reside within you. Relish the growth and harmony they bring to your being.

Look within and around you and celebrate the beauty of life. As our perception of life's true essence becomes more amplified, welcoming, living, and cherishing each moment follows naturally.

Congratulations!

You've successfully evolved from fear to freedom.

The magnitude of this moment, the radical understanding and metamorphosis of your fears, is immeasurable. Anchor yourself in the present, focusing on the cadence of your breath and the synchronicity of your Four Bodies. Bask in this intentional act of release and alignment. Celebrate the significance of this moment. Once you feel centered and prepared, we'll move forward.

CHAPTER 24
STEPPING INTO FREEDOM

With each fear confronted, we step closer to our authentic selves, flowing with the rhythm of the present moment.

The title of this book, *Transcending Anxiety: From Fear to Freedom,* made two clear promises. In Chapter 8, Shifting the Narrative, we addressed the first by bringing our unacknowledged fears into the light, effectively transcending anxiety. By applying The Mattain Five-Step Process in Chapter 23, we successfully transformed fear into freedom, upholding the second.

As we progress, our lens adjusts to focus on the immense power of the present moment. With the foundation we've established by deconstructing and reshaping fears through The Mattain Five-Step Process, we're poised to truly resonate with our present reality.

I'm sure you've come across teachings and spiritual guides that emphasize the value of being present. While the notion of living in the present isn't new, recognizing its power is crucial.

Let's unravel the paradox of the present moment: so powerful, yet so elusive.

- Why is the present moment so revered?

- What gives it so much potency?

- How might we tap into its infinite strength?

- And, if it holds such power, why does it remain unreachable to many of us, most of the time?

Let's continue our exploration, enhancing our connection to the enduring wisdom of the present.

SECTION III:
THE ESSENCE OF THE
PRESENT MOMENT

In the heartbeat of the present, unburdened by the past and undistracted by the future, we find the profound silence of existence.

CHAPTER 25
THE ESSENCE OF THE NOW

The power of The Mattain Five Steps lies in guiding you to embrace the expressions of your Four Bodies, allowing you to be present in the now. This is where the infinite power of life can be found.

Building on our exploration of fear and The Four Bodies, we now address the true solution to what we often call "anxiety." All aspects of fear we've examined underscore a key truth: in the context of anxiety, fear is deeply rooted in apprehensions about the *future* (whereas emotions like guilt and shame keep us tethered to the *past*). This fear stems from our uncertainty about what lies ahead and is amplified by our inability to control the unknown.

When we anchor ourselves firmly in the present moment, in the now, there's an absence of fear. We're met with the sheer beauty and majesty of life.

You might wonder, "Why didn't you simply advocate for being in the present from the outset?" The answer is layered.

If we're unable to connect with our Four Bodies because we're entrenched in PAINS—Projecting, Amplifying, Intellectualizing, Negating, and/or Suppressing—then achieving genuine presence becomes a daunting task.

Just imagine driving a car with warning lights flashing—low fuel, engine issues, a trail of smoke. Could you genuinely enjoy the scenic views around you? The chances are slim, as your immediate priority would be to find a solution or safety.

This doesn't mean you can't be present if something genuinely fearful is happening right now. Presence isn't only about experiencing pleasant sensations. If there's an immediate trigger for fear in your current reality—perhaps a difficult conversation you're in, a physical pain you're feeling, or yes, even a metaphorical (or literal!) bear—you can be present with it. Being aware of the fear, feeling its sensations in your Four Bodies, and allowing it to be without layering on future worries or past regrets is a powerful form of presence. The "flashing car lights" analogy best represents being overwhelmed by unacknowledged, past- or future-rooted resistance (PAINS-ing) that hinders our ability to see the present clearly.

In the same vein, if our Four Bodies are tense, our emotions neglected, our minds caught in relentless loops, and/or we feel overwhelmed by life, the prospect of savoring the simple joys around us, like the magnificent scent of blooming flowers or the melodic chirping of birds, is difficult.

When we're bound by identities like "anxiety" or beliefs such as "Life is a struggle," "I'm not good enough," or "My life is out of control," being present can feel like an insurmountable challenge.

This notion is why our focus thus far has been about shedding these restrictive identities and conceptions. We've engaged with The Mattain Five-Step Process, enabling us to connect, observe, respect, and even relish the expressions of our Four Bodies.

Now, equipped with new insights, we stand ready to absorb ourselves fully in the present.

The real magic of The Mattain Five Steps lies in its capacity to lead us towards accepting every expression of our Four Bodies, facilitating our ability to be authentically present in the now. Surrender represents the act of unconditionally embracing the present moment, regardless of its manifestations. It signifies the essence of The Unconditional Three: Worthiness, Love, and Freedom, achieved through ACT—Acceptance, Compassion, and Trust.

Mattain Moment 37: **The Sacred Gap**

I invite you to pause with me and savor what I call "the sacred gap"—that space of infinite potential accessible in the pauses at the top of your inhale and bottom of your exhale.

1. **Breathe In:** Take a slow, deep breath in, filling your lungs completely.

2. **Pause (Lungs Full):** Hold the breath gently for a moment with your lungs comfortably full. Focus on that brief pause between the inhale and the exhale. This pause is one doorway into the stillness of the sacred gap. Feel into that space. Recognize it as the place from which infinite beauty, silence, abundance, Worthiness, Love, and Freedom emanate.

3. **Breathe Out:** Now, exhale slowly and completely, releasing any tension, feeling your lungs empty gently.

4. **Pause (Lungs Empty):** Notice the brief, quiet stillness at the very bottom of the exhale, when your lungs are empty, just before your next inhale naturally begins. This pause is another doorway into that same sacred gap. Sense the potential held in this spacious emptiness.

5. **Repeat & Integrate:** Take two or three more full breath cycles like this. With each cycle, consciously notice how the same profound stillness of the sacred gap can be sensed in the brief pauses when the lungs are full and empty.

Relish the profound power held within the ever-present sacred gap, always accessible through your own breath.

By connecting with all Four Bodies, you've developed a mastery of diving inwards and harnessing the power to be present. This is the essence of what countless spiritual teachers have emphasized: the immense power of being in the now, the infinite potential of life.

You will soon possess the skills to not just get here but stay here. Life is most amazing in the now.

Congratulations! You've connected with the remarkable secret of the truth, beauty, and infinite nature of the now.

In the upcoming chapter, we'll probe further into the realm of presence. I'll introduce practical tools, exercises, and concepts to facilitate your ability to calibrate your Four Bodies and remain in the present. Mastering this art not only elevates your connection to the moment but also lays a foundation for inner power, joy, and a stronger connection to both yourself and your surroundings. Prepare to plunge into techniques that will strengthen your "muscles" of alignment and presence, grounding you in the intense power of the now.

CHAPTER 26
GETTING INTO THE NOW

Strengthen your "now" muscles, one conscious moment at a time.

We've explored the beauty of the present moment—the "now." We understand why it's the antidote to anxiety and the space where our true essence is found. But knowing why isn't the same as being there, right? Especially when the mind is racing, the body is tense, or old patterns (those pesky PAINS!) try to pull us into the past or future.

This chapter is all about the how.

You'll discover simple, practical tools—anchors, really—that you can use anytime, anywhere, to bring yourself back to the present. Presence isn't some mystical state reserved for gurus on mountaintops; it's your natural state of being, and these practices help you remember how to access it. Like any muscle, the more you practice toning it, the easier it gets. "It's hard, until it's not!"

The Breath: Your Constant Anchor

We touched on this briefly before, but let's dive deeper. Your breath is *always* with you, from your first moment to your last. It's your ultimate anchor to the present.

- **Simple Awareness:** Keep a soft gaze. Simply notice the sensations of your breath entering and leaving your body. Feel the rise and fall of your chest or abdomen. Don't try to change anything; just observe. When the mind wanders (and it will!), gently guide it back to the breath. Do this for about thirty seconds.

- **Counting Breaths:** For a more focused practice, count each exhale up to five or ten, then start again. Inhale... exhale (one)... inhale... exhale (two).... This practice gives the mind a simple task to keep you grounded.

- **The Sacred Gap:** Remember Mattain Moment 37: The Sacred Gap? Practice consciously noticing the sacred gap—that space of infinite potential—in the brief pauses after you fully inhale and after you fully exhale. This practice connects you to the stillness always accessible within your own breath cycle.

Sensory Grounding: Engaging Your Superpowers

Your physical senses are direct portals to the present moment. When your mind is spinning, ground yourself using your senses:

- **See:** Look around you. *Really* look. Notice three things you see right now. Observe their colors, shapes, and textures without labeling, just seeing.

- **Hear:** Listen intently. What sounds are present? Identify two distinct sounds, near or far, without interpreting.

- **Feel:** Bring awareness to one physical sensation *right now*. Notice the feeling of your feet on the floor, your hands resting on your lap, or the texture of your clothes against your skin.

- **Smell:** Take a breath in through your nose. What scents are present in the air, even subtly? What are their qualities? Notice without analyzing.

- **Taste:** Bring awareness to your mouth. Are there any lingering tastes, or simply a sensation within it? Observe without judgement.

Engaging your senses instantly pulls your awareness out of past/future thinking and into your immediate reality.

Body Awareness Lite: Feeling Your Inner Landscape

You can easily connect with your body through this quick check-in:

- Bring awareness to the feeling of aliveness within your body. Can you feel a subtle energy, a tingling, a warmth?

- Focus on your hands. Can you feel the spaces between your fingers?

- Focus on your feet. Can you feel them connected to the earth or the floor?

- Simply affirm: "I am here, in this body, right now." This exercise grounds you in your physical presence.

Mindful Action: Presence in Motion

Integrate presence into your day by bringing awareness to simple activities.

- **Washing Dishes:** Feel the warmth of the water, the texture of the sponge; notice the bubbles and slipperiness of the soap, the movement of your hands.

- **Walking:** Feel your feet making contact with the ground, the air on your skin, the movement of your body through space.

- **Drinking Tea/Coffee:** Notice the warmth of the mug, the aroma, the taste, the sensations of swallowing.

- **Eating:** Enjoy the scents, colors, textures, and tastes of your food. Savor each bite and the sensations of chewing and swallowing.

- **Brushing/Flossing Teeth:** Feel the bristles or thread against your teeth and gums, indulge in the taste of the toothpaste or floss, and notice the sensations of cleaning and rinsing.

Choose one activity each day and commit to bringing your full, non-judgmental awareness to it. This routine trains your mind to focus on the present moment.

Observing Thoughts: Clouds in the Sky

As we seek to immerse ourselves in the present, the goal isn't to stop thinking, but to stop *identifying* with every thought.

- Imagine your thoughts are clouds floating across the vast blue sky of your awareness.

- When a thought arises (worry, planning, judgement), simply label it gently: "Ah, thinking," or "There's worry."

- Let the thought-cloud drift by without getting caught up in its story or needing to follow it, change it, or determine its origins.

- Remember: You are the sky, not the clouds.

Mattain Moment 38: **Feeling What's Here Now**

Tuning into your Emotional Body brings you into the present. Let's practice simply being aware of and allowing whatever emotion is here right now.

1. **Pause & Tune In:** Take a breath. Gently bring your awareness inward.

2. **Identify the Emotion:** Ask yourself quietly, "What emotion am I feeling right now?" Don't search hard; just notice the most obvious feeling present, even if it's subtle (like boredom, restlessness, irritation, contentment, or calmness).

3. **Name It (Gently):** Silently name the emotion without evaluation: "Okay, feeling restless." "Ah, peace." "Okay, frustration is here." "I feel grateful right now."

4. **Locate It (Bodily Awareness):** Where does this feeling seem to live in your body right now? Your chest? Stomach? Shoulders? Head? Just notice. If it's in more than one area, see if you can localize its center.

5. **Allow (Don't Resist):** Breathe *with* the feeling for a few moments. Can you simply *allow* it to be there, exactly as it is, without needing to change it, fix it, or push it away? Just offer it space.

This simple act of noticing and allowing your current emotional state brings you directly into the present moment, freeing you from the resistance that fuels anxiety.

Recognizing Your Natural Presence

Now, you might be thinking, "Okay Manal, breath-work, sensory scans... that sounds like conscious effort!" But guess what? You've already experienced deep presence without even labeling it. And it's natural and easy for you to do so.

Think about those activities where time just seems to melt away. Where you're completely absorbed, focused, maybe even feeling a sense of joy or effortless flow. Perhaps it's running, getting lost in a good book, knitting intricate patterns, painting, playing an instrument, gardening, cooking a familiar meal, solving a tricky crossword, lifting weights at the gym, or even deep coding. That feeling of being completely immersed, "in the zone?" **That, my friends, *is* presence!**

These activities naturally quiet mental chatter because your focus is engaged in the activity itself. In other words, when your mind is wholly here, it can't be elsewhere! You're anchored firmly in the *doing*, in the *being*, in the *moment*, leaving little room for past regrets or future anxieties to take hold.

Mattain Moment 39: **Your Flow Activities**

What activities already bring you into this state of natural presence or flow? Identify one or two right now. Acknowledge them.

Next time you're engaged in one, bring a conscious awareness to the feeling of being present. Notice the ease, the focus, the lack of mental noise. Savor the moment. Smile.

Dealing with a Wandering Mind (With Compassion!)

Your mind *will* wander. That's its job! When you notice it's drifted off during any of these practices, don't get frustrated or judge yourself. That's just more resistance! Simply, gently, and *compassionately* acknowledge where the mind went ("Ah, planning again!") and guide your awareness back to your chosen anchor (breath, senses, body). Think of it like training a playful puppy or kitten—gentle redirection, again and again, with kindness.

Integration into Daily Life

Start small. Choose one or two of these practices that resonate with you. Try incorporating them into your day for just a minute or two at a time. Consider setting a few daily alarms—you could even label each as a "Mattain Moment"—as reminders to pause. Consistency is key. The more you practice anchoring yourself in the now, the more natural it becomes, and the more you'll experience the peace, clarity, and joy that reside there.

This consistent practice strengthens your "muscles" of alignment and presence, centering you in the intense beauty and power of the now.

SECTION IV:
ALCHEMY FOR ALIGNMENT

In the journey of self-discovery, every layer of understanding, every moment of awareness, adds to the alchemy of transformation.

CHAPTER 27
BUILDING THE MUSCLES
OF ALIGNMENT

Just as our physical muscles are shaped by consistent effort and time, so too are the muscles of The Four Bodies sculpted by every conscious moment we embrace.

Throughout this book, we've navigated alignment, presence, and surrender, among many other states of being. This section introduces strategies to further strengthen the "muscles" of your Four Bodies, enabling you to inhabit a state of surrender more deeply and consistently.

Many set out on self-discovery quests, armed with self-help books and teachings, only to encounter moments of frustration. Moments when old patterns return, when progress appears elusive. Many of us know these sentiments all too well: "I thought I'd overcome this!" or "I thought I'd learned that lesson."

View these moments as set-points rather than setbacks. They offer opportunities to measure our growth, recalibrate, and move forward with even greater focus and wisdom.

It's valuable to remember that we've spent decades, perhaps even lifetimes, forming the patterns we're now working to change. As we engage with exercises and strategies to strengthen our spiritual and mental muscles, let's do so with immense compassion for ourselves. It took years for you to arrive at this current point; honor the time it takes to calibrate back to The Unconditional Three.

For a long time, I wished I knew all these tools years ago; they would have provided the self-compassion I so desperately needed as I found my truth. I was habitually frustrated and self-judgmental.

However, one day, it dawned on me: Had I known then what I know now, I wouldn't have been the person I was, nor evolved into the person I am today. This idea bathed me in genuine compassion for every stage of my existence. I invite you to unearth the truth that guides you to alignment through ACTS: Acceptance, Compassion, Trust, and ultimately, Surrender, on your own timeline.

We've all heard the saying, "It's about the journey, not the destination." While it may sound cliché, its truth is profound. When we embrace this wisdom, the essence of the journey becomes revolutionary. The destination, while important, is but a point in time; the journey, on the other hand, is where life truly unfolds.

In the next four chapters, I'll focus on practical ways to strengthen and coordinate The Four Bodies. This time, we'll start with the Physical Body and work our way up through the Emotional, Mental, and Egoic. You might wonder why this sequence differs from the order presented in Part I. In Part I, my approach was to build from the top down. Here, with the foundations now laid, we'll construct from the bottom up.

Expanding on this thought leads to an age-old conundrum: Which came first, the chicken or the egg? Likewise, where does alignment truly begin? Does well-being primarily flow "bottom-up"—starting from our Physical Body and influencing our Emotional, Mental, and Egoic states? Or does it flow "top-down"—originating from our Egoic beliefs and shaping our Mental, Emotional, and Physical realities? While this debate has no single "correct" answer, as the influence moves in both directions, what's clear is the importance of both ends of this spectrum. A robust Physical Body provides a grounded foundation, supporting bottom-up harmony and resilience. Similarly, an aligned Egoic

Body, rooted in truth, provides clear direction for top-down coherence and purpose. The core message remains: all Four Bodies are integral and deeply integrated in the experience of alignment.

For each Body, the first step is Awareness of its nature and expressions. Then, there are ways to fortify each Body.

This section was fun for me to investigate, and I hope that you enjoy it equally. Celebrate every moment and every step of progress. Let's get started!

CHAPTER 28
ACCEPTANCE IN THE PHYSICAL BODY

Our physical well-being is the foundation upon which our mental, emotional, and egoic wellness thrives.

This section holds special significance for me. For years, my journey was marked by a persistent "struggle" with body image and navigating overwhelming fatigue. This personal pursuit of understanding my physical well-being began in my early teens—a time when I, like many, explored, examined, and cried and laughed along with Oprah and Phil Donahue (I'm showing my age here!), trying to make sense of all things human. It was this deep dive into my own physical experience that eventually illuminated my profound connection to overall wholeness.

Here, I highlight the intricate ways in which our Physical Body influences our Four Bodies. The foundation of alignment in the Physical Body lies in acceptance.

Many of us have been conditioned to judge ourselves for our physical appearances, the lives we've led, and the choices we've made. Society and ingrained conditioning perpetuate assumptions that unless we meet specific aesthetic standards or our lives follow a pre-defined trajectory, we're somehow unworthy. Such perspectives have led many of us to unconsciously harbor resentment, particularly towards our bodies. Overcoming this conditioning requires an unwavering commitment to acceptance: towards ourselves, our bodies, and our stories.

Embrace the unfolding of your life as your unique, evolving narrative, seeing "mistakes" and "failures" not as definitions of who you are, but as mere stepping stones along the way.

A vital part of fortifying the Physical Body is the acceptance of self, body, mind, emotions, and life experiences. This ideal is the essence of The Mattain philosophy—finding that sacred space of Acceptance, Compassion, and Trust for physical experience, and ultimately, for the entirety of your being. In this nurturing environment, the seed of your true self can sprout, free from the shackles of judgement and resistance, and blossom into a life that is authentically and unconditionally *yours*. This is what it tastes like to yield truly to life.

Daily habits—from our diet and physical activity to sleep quality and hydration patterns—impact all aspects of our being: Physical, Emotional, Mental, and Egoic.

The Physical Body frequently presents a substantial roadblock, becoming a crucial hurdle on the road to wholeness. Physiological aspects contribute to resistance, influencing how we interpret interactions with ourselves and the world around us. Our subsequent discussion will detail these elements in depth, highlighting the complex ways through which the Physical Body contributes to harmony.

While I don't claim expertise in human physiology, my own journey underscores the vital role of physical health in overall wellness. I cover these topics, significant in my personal saga, from a perspective shared with love and authenticity. The goal here is to nurture awareness, respect, and love for every facet of our physical selves, discerning the physiological aspects that may amplify expressions in our Four Bodies. Understanding, indeed, liberates.

In this chapter, I return to using the term "anxiety." In mainstream descriptions, anxiety connotes a medical diagnosis. My use of the term aims to resonate with the everyday language people use to describe feelings of stress and unease, but I urge you to recall our unique lens on employing this label.

The central premise is that anxiety is an expression of discomfort across our Four Bodies. It signals that something is out of balance and calls for our attention.

When we talk about anxiety in this context, remember that it's not about labeling ourselves with a condition. Instead, it's about recognizing how our life experiences shape our Four Bodies. By addressing these manifestations, we can foster a state of health and well-being that supports our evolution of transcending fear and embracing Worthiness, Love, and Freedom.

Let's start with a subject close to all our hearts (and our tummies!): food.

You Are What You Eat

The phrase "You are what you eat" holds significant truth. The food we consume fuels our Four Bodies, affecting our physical health, emotional well-being,[8] as well as mental[9] and egoic states. Studies have shown a correlation between diet and mental health, with certain foods contributing to heightened anxiety and fear.[10] Honoring our bodies' unique needs and responses to different foods and drinks is crucial for maintaining a healthy mind-body balance.

We must also consider the impacts of food intolerances and allergies, the effects of alcohol, drugs, caffeine, supplements, and medications, and the roles of sugar and gut health. Another important factor to consider is that what our body needs can, and will, vary over time.

Over what feels like my whole lifetime, I've devoted time and effort to listening to my body and discovering what it needs to be efficiently fueled. I've taken numerous tests to learn about food intolerances and allergies, unearthing a strong connection between physical health and the food and drink I consume.

---

[8] Firth J., Gangwisch J.E., Borisini A., Wootton R.E., Mayer E.A. "Food and Mood: How Do Diet and Nutrition Affect Mental Wellbeing?" BMJ. 2020 Jun 29; 369:m2382. doi: 10.1136/bmj.m2382. Body Mind Journal. 2020 Nov 9;371:m4269. doi: 10.1136/bmj.m4269. PMID: 32601102; PMCID: PMC7322666.

[9] Gheonea T.C., Oancea C.N., Mititelu M., Lupu E.C., Ioniță-Mindrican C.B., Rogoveanu I. "Nutrition and Mental Well-Being: Exploring Connections and Holistic Approaches." Journal of Clinical Medicine. 2023 Nov 20;12(22):7180. doi: 10.3390/jcm12227180. PMID: 38002792; PMCID: PMC10672474.

[10] Aucoin M., LaChance L., Naidoo U., Remy D., Shekdar T., Sayar N., Cardozo V., Rawana T., Chan I., Cooley K. "Diet and Anxiety: A Scoping Review." Nutrients. 2021 Dec 10;13(12):4418. doi: 10.3390/nu13124418. PMID: 34959972; PMCID: PMC8706568.

Time further uncovers a fascinating relationship with food. The essence of this idea is in identifying your feelings before, during, and after you eat. For instance, how do you feel before, during, and after indulging in something you perceive as "unhealthy," maybe a donut, ice cream, or piece of cake? Then, notice how those feelings contrast with the sensations you feel after consuming a meal you deem "healthy." You may wish to keep a Food and Mood Log that helps you track not only what you eat and when, but also how you feel before, during, and afterwards.

Keep in mind that the impact of the food you eat—whether it's an apple or a donut—extends far beyond the moment you finish it; the "after" can be felt that same evening, days, months, or even years later. The consequences of dietary patterns, such as clogged arteries, high blood pressure, or blood sugar imbalances from years of certain choices, or conversely, the profound benefits of a consistently nourishing diet, often take weeks, months, or years to fully manifest. Recognizing these long-term connections requires a high level of sustained awareness and objectivity.

Choosing what to consume to optimize your health is not one-size-fits-all, and what works best for you might not work as well for another. I encourage you to navigate your own voyage of self-discovery—get to know your Physical Body, health, and diet. Uncover the unique balance that works for you and have fun discovering the optimal fuel to supercharge your life.

Understanding your body's unique needs and responses to food can make a significant difference in your path of transcending fear. Regularly consuming a balanced, nutrient-rich diet and avoiding foods that trigger inflammation or intolerances can contribute to improved mental clarity and emotional balance. Many people find value, particularly as they age, in the anti-inflammatory diet for this reason.[11] You may wish to consult a nutritionist/dietician to determine the best regimen for you.

---

[11] "Anti-Inflammatory Diet." Johns Hopkins Medicine, www.hopkinsmedicine.org/health/wellness-and-prevention/an-

The Importance of Gut Health

Along my road to wellness and wholeness, I've ventured into the subject of gut health. Our gut health plays a critical role in our overall wellness. It's been said that the gut is the second brain,[12] and indeed, a strong connection exists between our digestive health and our mental and emotional states.

The gut and brain are physically and biochemically connected, primarily through the vagus nerve,[13] paving the way for continuous communication. This connection is so strong that our gut microbiome—the community of bacteria living in our intestines—has been found to influence mood and mental health. Supporting this connection is key; practices aimed at improving vagal tone, such as deep, slow breathing (4-in, 6-out count), humming, or certain types of gentle movement can positively influence this pathway.

Poor gut health can exhibit in numerous ways, including food intolerances and allergies, inflammation, and a condition known as "leaky gut." While the term "leaky gut" isn't universally accepted in mainstream medicine, the underlying concept aligns with my understanding of the body's interconnectedness and my personal health. Leaky gut, or increased intestinal permeability, may lead to a myriad of health issues, including mental health problems.[14]

---

ti-inflammatory-diet.

[12] Ruder, Debra Bradley. "The Gut and the Brain." Harvard Medical School, 2017, hms.harvard.edu/news-events/publications-archive/brain/gut-brain#:~:text=The%20enteric%20nervous%20system%20that,brain%20when%20something%20is%20amiss.

[13] Han Y.., Wang B., Gao H., He C., Hua R., Liang C., Zhang S., Wang Y., Xin S., Xu J. "Vagus Nerve and Underlying Impact on the Gut Microbiota-Brain Axis in Behavior and Neurodegenerative Diseases." Journal of Inflammatory Research. 2022 Nov 9;15:6213-6230. doi: 10.2147/JIR.S384949. PMID: 36386584; PMCID: PMC9656367.

[14] Sharp, Loretta Graziano. "Mind Your Theta: Achieving Theta Activity Through Meditation." Psychology Today, Sussex Publishers, 24 Jan. 2022, www.psychologytoday.com/us/blog/your-neurology/202201/mind-your-theta-achieving-theta-activity-meditation.

Understanding your body's unique needs and responses to food can make a significant difference as you strive to transcend anxiety. Supporting your gut microbiome generally involves:

1. Consuming a balanced, nutrient-rich diet focusing on whole foods. A diverse array of fibrous whole foods, including broccoli stems, asparagus, dark leafy greens, beans, whole seeds, and fruit peels, provides excellent nourishment for gut bacteria.[15]

2. Incorporating sources of *prebiotics* (fibers that feed beneficial bacteria, like those found in onions, garlic, asparagus, and bananas) and *probiotics* (live beneficial bacteria found in fermented foods or supplements).[16]

3. Considering digestive *food enzymes*, if needed, under guidance of a nutritionist or healthcare provider.[17]

4. Identifying and minimizing foods that trigger inflammation or intolerances for *you*.

I'd like to note that while *fermented foods* (like kimchi, sauerkraut, and kefir) are excellent sources of probiotics for many, they may not be suitable for everyone, particularly individuals with histamine intolerance or conditions like Mast Cell Activation Syndrome (MCAS).[18] Always listen to your body, consult a healthcare provider and/or nutritionist, and consider personalization.

---

[15] McLean Hospital, "Diet and Mental Health: How Nutrition Shapes Your Well-Being," May 24, 2024. https://www. mcleanhospital.org/essential/nutrition.

[16] Al-Habsi N., Al-Khalili M., Haque S.A., Elias M., Olqi N.A., Al Uraimi T. "Health Benefits of Prebiotics, Probiotics, Synbiotics, and Postbiotics." Nutrients. 2024 Nov 19;16(22):3955. doi: 10.3390/nu16223955. PMID: 39599742; PMCID: PMC11597603.

[17] Denhard, Morgan, MS, RD, LDN. "Digestive Enzymes and Digestive Enzyme Supplements." Johns Hopkins Medicine, www.hopkinsmedicine.org/health/wellness-and-prevention/digestive-enzymes-and-digestive-enzyme-supplements.

[18] Barnett, Oliver. "Do I Have Mast Cell Activation Syndrome?" London Clinic of Nutrition, londonclinicofnutrition. co.uk/nutrition-articles/do-i-have-mast-cell-activation-syndrome/#:~:text=A%20common%20approach%20to%20 MCAS,dairy:%20cheese%2C%20yoghurt%2C%20kefir. Accessed 7 May 2025.

Improving gut health can contribute significantly to improved mental clarity, emotional balance, and overall resilience.

The Thyroid: The Body's Metabolic Conductor

I've come to discover the remarkable power of the thyroid. In the previous section, I mentioned that some regard the gut as the second brain. Similarly, within the context of holistic health, I identify what might be termed the "four brains": the stomach, heart, thyroid, and brain. This notion has expanded my appreciation for the intricate connections among these "centers" and their collective impact on our well-being.

These interconnected organs—the thyroid, stomach, heart, and brain—work synergistically to support our overall health and well-being, with each playing a unique role in fostering wellness.

The thyroid, a butterfly-shaped gland located in the neck, is often referred to as the body's metabolic conductor. This gland plays a vital role in regulating our metabolism, energy levels, body temperature, and even mood. Thyroid hormones interact with many cells in the body and have a significant impact on our overall sense of well-being.[19]

When the thyroid is out of balance, it can give rise to conditions such as hypothyroidism (underactive thyroid), hyperthyroidism (overactive thyroid),[20] or Hashimoto's disease—an autoimmune condition of the thyroid.[21] These conditions can result in a range of symptoms including fatigue, weight fluctuations, mood swings, anxiety, and depression.[22]

---

[19] "Thyroid." Cleveland Clinic, my.clevelandclinic.org/health/body/23188-thyroid.

[20] Sievert, Diane. "Hypothyroidism vs. Hyperthyroidism: What's the Difference?" UCLA Health, medschool.ucla.edu/news-article/hypothyroidism-vs-hyperthyroidism-whats-the-difference.

[21] "Hashimoto's Thyroiditis." Johns Hopkins Medicine, www.hopkinsmedicine.org/health/conditions-and-diseases/hashimotos-thyroiditis.

[22] "Thyroid disease: Can it cause mood swings?" Mayo Clinic, www.mayoclinic.org/diseases-conditions/hyperthyroidism/expert-answers/thyroid-disease/faq-20058228.

For some, an imbalance in thyroid function can be a root cause of their fear or anxiety symptoms.[23] By addressing thyroid health through proper nutrition, lifestyle modifications, and medical interventions, when necessary, we can optimize our body's performance and, subsequently, our mental and emotional health.[24]

You may wish to work with a physician, functional medicine provider, and/or naturopath to get your own thyroid and other hormone levels tested.

Moving Towards Balance: The Power of Exercise

Physical activity is another essential component of holistic health. Regular exercise can boost mood, reduce stress, improve sleep, and enhance cognitive function[25]—all of which can positively impact our experiences of fear and anxiety.

Exercise stimulates the release of endorphins and other feel-good hormones that promote feelings of happiness and well-being.[26]

We are all so aware of the benefits of exercise, so it's not necessary to go into detail here. There is no one right way to practice this form of physical nourishment. Some forms of exercise you may enjoy include mindful stretching, such as yoga or Tai Chi; aerobic exercise (cardio), such as running, swimming, or biking; muscle-building activities like weightlifting or calisthenics; and even just a walk around the block.

---

[23] "Psychological Symptoms and Thyroid Disorders." British Thyroid Foundation, www.btf-thyroid.org/psychological-symptoms-and-thyroid-disorders.

[24] Shulhai A.M., Rotondo R., Petraroli M., Patianna V., Predieri B., Iughetti L., Esposito S., Street M.E. "The Role of Nutrition on Thyroid Function." Nutrients. 2024 Jul 31;16(15):2496. doi: 10.3390/nu16152496. PMID: 39125376; PMCID: PMC11314468.

[25] Mahindru A., Patil P., Agrawal V. "Role of Physical Activity on Mental Health and Well-Being: A Review." Cureus. 2023 Jan 7;15(1):e33475. doi: 10.7759/cureus.33475. PMID: 36756008; PMCID: PMC9902068.

[26] Mayo Clinic Staff. "Exercise and stress: Get moving to manage stress." Mayo Clinic, Mayo Foundation for Medical Education and Research, 6 May 2023, www.mayoclinic.org/healthy-lifestyle/stress-management/in-depth/exercise-and-stress/art-20044469. Accessed 7 May 2025.

Personally, I am a lover of yoga, long walks in Umstead State Park, and most recently, strength training to complement the aging process. Regarding anxiety, note that *excessive*, intense, high-impact exercise can elevate cortisol, potentially exacerbating feelings of overwhelm and stress.[27] Be mindful to consult a healthcare provider before engaging in any type of exercise to determine the best regimen that fits your needs.

The Healing Power of Sleep

Adequate, quality sleep is a frequently overlooked yet integral aspect of overall health and well-being. During sleep, our bodies grow and repair, while our brains process memories. Poor sleep can lead to impaired cognitive function, compromised immune function, and an increased risk of developing metabolic diseases.[28] Sleep problems can also lead to anxiety and depression.[29]

Prioritizing sleep—ensuring both its quality and quantity—can significantly impact our emotional resilience and ability to manage fear.

To improve your nightly rest, The National Sleep Foundation offers a range of strategies. You may consider going to bed and waking up at the same time every day, listening to relaxing music before bed, maintaining a cool sleep environment, using blackout curtains/shades, limiting caffeine (especially later in the day), and/or reducing alcohol/nicotine.[30]

Personally, I use a smart ring that tracks my sleep quality and activity levels and provides a "readiness" score reflecting my body's recovery. As a self-proclaimed nerdy engineer, I find having this quantitative data incredibly helpful for tracking my wellness. I also use a sleep-monitoring bed that provides daily, weekly, and

---

[27] Healthline Editorial Team. "The Cortisol Creep: What Is It and How to Avoid It?" Healthline, Healthline Media, 2 Nov. 2022, https://www.healthline.com/health/fitness/the-cortisol-creep#What-is-cortisol.
[28] Caldwell, Alison. "How Sleep Affects Human Health, Explained." University of Chicago News, https://news.uchicago.edu/explainer/how-sleep-affects-human-health-explained. 2024.
[29] Zakarin, Elizabeth Blake. "How Sleep Deprivation Impacts Mental Health." Columbia University Department of Psychiatry, 16 Mar. 2022, https://www.columbiapsychiatry.org/news/how-sleep-deprivation-affects-your-mental-health.
[30] "Sleep Tips." National Sleep Foundation, thensf.org/sleep-tips/. 2025.

monthly sleep scores. This information helps me make informed choices about my activities to cultivate healthy sleep patterns. For me, technology is a great complement to intuitively feeling my way towards wellness. I encourage you to explore how technology could help you monitor your patterns and guide you in establishing positive habits.

Hydration: The Elixir of Life

Staying adequately hydrated is essential for our physical health, which in turn impacts our mental and emotional states. Water is vital for nearly every bodily function, including carrying nutrients to cells, flushing toxins out of the body, and even protecting organs.[31]

Severe dehydration has significant consequences, emphasizing the impact hydration has on our Four Bodies (even if we can't always see it directly). Dehydration can lead to a multitude of health issues, including fatigue, headaches, and confusion.[32] Ensuring we consume enough water daily can support our overall health and aid in our expedition of breaking free from fear.

According to the Mayo Clinic, general guidelines suggest men drink about 15.5 cups of water (3.7 liters) a day, and women 11.5 cups (2.7 liters). However, these are just estimates; individual needs vary by health, activity levels, and climate.[33] Personally, I gauge my optimal-hydration by listening to my body—how I feel, bathroom frequency, and urine quality (does you reading it feel as funny as me writing it?). Humor aside, it's a surprisingly practical gauge; I find I can use the color, smell, and quantity of my urine as clear indicators of how hydrated or dehydrated I may be. I encourage you to step into awareness and discover the hydration level that feels best for your body.

[31] [25] Wergin, Allie. "Water: Essential for Your Body." Mayo Clinic Health System, 29 Sep. 2022, https://www.mayoclinichealthsystem.org/hometown-health/speaking-of-health/water-essential-to-your-body-video.

[32] "Dehydration." Cleveland Clinic, https://my.clevelandclinic.org/health/diseases/9013-dehydration. Accessed 4 Apr. 2025.

[33] Mayo Clinic Staff. "Water: How Much Should You Drink Every Day?" Mayo Clinic, Mayo Foundation for Medical Education and Research, 12 Oct. 2022, https://www.mayoclinic.org/healthy-lifestyle/nutrition-and-healthy-eating/in-depth/water/art-20044256.

Water quality is another important factor for overall wellness. Water quality varies significantly by jurisdiction, region,[34] and country;[35] regulatory standards for acceptable drinking water don't always align with what's optimal for health. Because of this, I recently installed a whole-house water filtration system to reduce chlorine and other impurities. It's worth considering the quality of the water you use daily, both for drinking and showering, and researching options available in your area. You may want to get your water tested by a reputable company, too.

Neurofeedback: Balancing the Brain

The functionality of our brain can be influenced by a variety of factors, including concussions, medical conditions, and even everyday occurrences. Sometimes, these factors can lead to physiological imbalances that may alter our mood, cognition, and overall well-being. Neurofeedback is a powerful tool that can help address these imbalances.

Neurofeedback is a non-invasive process that uses real-time displays of brain activity—typically through electroencephalography (EEG)—to teach self-regulation of brain functions. This method can be beneficial for managing anxiety.[36]

Neurofeedback has been used to treat a wide range of conditions, including ADHD, anxiety, depression, post-traumatic stress disorder (PTSD), migraines, sleep disorders, and more. However, its application isn't limited to addressing medical conditions; it can also optimize brain performance.

---

[34] "Ground Water and Drinking Water." United States Environmental Protection Agency, www.epa.gov/ground-water-and-drinking-water.

[35] "Drinking-Water Quality Guidelines." World Health Organization, www.who.int/teams/environment-climate-change-and-health/water-sanitation-and-health/water-safety-and-quality/drinking-water-quality-guidelines.

[36] Marzbani H., Marateb H.R., Mansourian M. "Neurofeedback: A Comprehensive Review on System Design, Methodology and Clinical Applications." Basic Clin Neurosci. 2016 Apr;7(2):143-58. doi: 10.15412/J.BCN.03070208. PMID: 27303609; PMCID: PMC4892319.

Athletes, executives,[37] and even NASA astronauts use neurofeedback training to improve their mental acuity and performance.[38]

I've had the opportunity to undergo neurofeedback myself. It was fascinating to note the direct correlations between my brain waves and physical state. There were days when I couldn't relax, when my alpha/theta waves wouldn't cross over during alpha-theta training (in neurofeedback speak, a concrete representation of the fact I couldn't relax). These periods were directly related to times I didn't take care of my body—for example, when I consumed foods that my body doesn't tolerate, like gluten. My mood was poor, and I felt off.

However, when I adhered to a diet more compatible with my body, the alpha/theta crossover during training was more consistent, leading to a noticeable improvement in my mood and overall well-being. This anecdote demonstrates the major impact that our dietary and lifestyle choices can have on our brain's physiological functioning and, in turn, our emotions and mental state. It's fascinating to witness how our Four Bodies reflect our brain's physiological functioning.

Additional Modalities for Ease

Beyond the core habits I've touched on, my own journey towards physical alignment has led me to explore various complementary practices, and I've found incredible value in many. Simple heat therapy, like relaxing in a hot tub, works wonders for muscle comfort. More recently, I jumped on the cold plunge bandwagon and have been amazed by the results—my Oura Ring consistently validates a significant increase in my "readiness" score after just 3 to 5 minutes in the cold plunge, and I've noticed considerable decreases in stress and inflammation. I've also explored the benefits of infrared sauna,

---

[37] Clasen, Sally. "Neurofeedback: The Future of Leadership Training." W. P. Carey News, 29 Oct. 2018.
[38] Neuronetix. "Harnessing the Brain and the Mind: NASA's Neurofeedback Training for Astronauts." Neuronetix, 28 Jun 2023.

red light therapy, and salt therapy for relaxation, as well as acupuncture and chiropractic care for energetic and structural balance. And of course, nothing beats an amazing massage! Listening to your body and discovering which additional modalities resonate with you can be an exciting part of supporting your Physical Body.

Addressing the physiological aspects of our body plays a significant role in our capability of managing fear and anxiety. Adopting a holistic approach to wellness lays the groundwork for moving past fear and advancing towards a state of Worthiness, Love, and Freedom. Let's now turn our attention to the Emotional Body.

CHAPTER 29
COMPASSION IN THE
EMOTIONAL BODY

Our emotions are the gateway to profound love and understanding within.

We've arrived at the Emotional Body, where compassion is central. In today's world, we're acutely attuned to our physical and mental states, yet our Emotional and Egoic Bodies often remain overshadowed. Rising discussions on emotional intelligence (EQ) and emotional awareness indicate a pivotal shift; their importance is increasingly featured in conversations about relationship compatibility, for example. We're collectively beginning to recognize the significance of our Emotional Bodies.

In this section, my primary goal is to highlight the necessity of actively nurturing awareness of your Emotional Body. A primary message of this book is to honor, respect, and cherish your emotional feedback system, to see it and appreciate it as the command center of your holistic self.

How do you nurture your emotional feedback system? By relishing joy in all aspects of life. Take pleasure in all of your actions and remember that you are a being of light. Approach life with inspiration. Know that we are meant for happiness and wholeness. Nourish potent love and compassion for every facet of life.

True compassion emerges when we appreciate that everyone is doing their best given the unique circumstances of their lives. Having discovered that life unfolds in countless ways, I define our collective journey as "humaning." This realization of our shared humanness enhances our emotional resilience, closing the distances between us.

Sympathy, Empathy, and Compassion

To foster genuine connection, clarifying the nature of emotional responses is essential. We must differentiate between sympathy, empathy, and compassion, as each has its own qualities.

Sympathy: Sympathy is an expression of feeling "sorry" for oneself or others. I view it as compassion infused with expressions of the ego; this perspective is because the feeling of sympathy, when extended to oneself or others, is tinged with undertones of "not good enough," "weakness," or "victimhood." I noticed when I expressed sympathy for others or situations, I sought to hide from my own anger. More than that, I realized it frequently involved my ego feeling superior, looking down on the situation rather than connecting with shared vulnerability or true compassion. Sympathy has its place, and if it's what you can express for a particular situation, that's perfectly okay.

Empathy: With empathy, we resonate *with* the feelings of another. If they're sad, we feel their sadness; if they're angry, we sense their anger. Its profound importance is undeniable; indeed, a significant lack of empathy is a hallmark of conditions like psychopathy, highlighting how essential it is for healthy human connection. While empathy beautifully captures the essence of our shared humanity and may help us feel close to someone (and them to us), it doesn't necessarily elevate the situation on its own. Because empathy involves mirroring the existing emotion, it can sometimes keep both people anchored in that feeling (e.g., staying sad together) or even pull the empathic person down emotionally, rather than lifting both people up. If empathy is the best you can offer in a situation, that's still fantastic, as it's an important human trait.

Compassion: Compassion is an amplified sentiment that emanates love, uplifting experiences for all involved. It stands as the highest form of expression of love.

While both sympathy and empathy are essential human responses, I advocate for nurturing your capacity for compassion, recognizing it as the most elevated form of emotional connection.

Mastering the art of connecting with our emotions and their deeper meanings is the liberation we all seek. So, how can we transition from emotions like sympathy and empathy, or resistant feelings, to true compassion?

A practical act towards strengthening the Emotional Body is the art of body scanning. While this meditative technique is typically applied to the Physical Body, you can adapt it to tune into the Emotional Body.

For example, when an emotion like "shame" surges, observe its physical footprint within your body, tracing its route from your extremities to your core. By tuning into sensations, you can gain valuable epiphanies as to how your emotions physically materialize within you and develop a better understanding as to their root.

Another invaluable tool is The Mattain Five Steps. This process allows you to examine the integrated expressions of your Four Bodies: Physical, Emotional, Mental, and Egoic. Deconstruct the Key Lime Pie and understand your Emotional Body's sentiments.

Appreciation and Gratitude

And don't forget to tap into the power of appreciation as a vehicle for emotional wholeness. By immersing yourself in authentic, felt appreciation, you invite waves of contentment and joy, nurturing the heart. However, it's important to distinguish this embodied appreciation from merely intellectualizing gratitude. Simply going through the motions of saying you're thankful, without truly feeling it deep within, can sometimes backfire, paradoxically bringing underlying resentment or a sense of inauthenticity to the surface.

If you find it challenging to connect with appreciation for specific personal circumstances, try starting with what feels more general and unwavering. For example, cultivating appreciation for the beauty and mystery of God, The Universe, the Earth, and Nature can often be a more readily accessible and steady source of genuine feeling. Sometimes, finding consistent appreciation for the "human" things in our lives can be a bit harder to regulate or keep steady—just ask anyone who's been married for over 20 years or is parenting a child going rogue (lol)! The goal is to resonate with appreciation across all Four Bodies.

Laughter

Lastly, there's one remedy, often overlooked in discussions about emotional well-being, that deserves our attention: laughter. A universal language of joy, laughter radiates pleasure across our Physical, Emotional, Mental, and Egoic spheres. I've had the privilege of hosting numerous live events titled "Laughter as a Tool for Healing." The collective joy felt during these sessions was truly remarkable.

Humor, in all forms, engages our Four Bodies in a dance of joy. While slapstick addresses the overt and physical, dry humor or wit requires our mind to discern nuanced ironies and layers. The allure of dry humor, which necessitates a keen intellect to fully appreciate, underscores the elegance of our Mental Body. Such intellectual playfulness showcases the vast potential and richness our minds hold. Consider the difference: the immediate, broad comedy of Jim Carrey or the classic slapstick of Charlie Chaplin engages us physically, while the deadpan delivery of Steve Carell (in certain roles) or the sharp, observational humor of Jerry Seinfeld requires mental engagement to appreciate.

Mattain Moment 40: **Sparking Joy with Laughter**

Ready to try a little laughter experiment? It might feel silly at first (most powerful things do!), but let's tap into this universal language of joy.

1. **Get Comfy:** Sit comfortably in your chair. You can place your hands gently on your knees or even on your belly to feel the movement.

2. **Start the Sound:** Now, begin making laughing sounds. Seriously! Maybe a subtle "ha-ha-ha," soft "hee-hee," or deeper "ho-ho-ho." Don't worry about it feeling real initially—just make the sound.

3. **Keep it Going (Gently!):** Continue making the sound for 30-60 seconds. Let the rhythm build naturally. If genuine chuckles or belly laughs want to emerge, let them! (I tend to find myself laughing just thinking about laughing! I even laughed writing this section, and every time I re-read it in the editing phase; I'm laughing right now!)

4. **Pause & Notice:** Okay, delicately pause. Take a breath. Tune into your Four Bodies.

   ° *Physical:* Any lightness? Vibrations? Less tension?

   ° *Emotional:* An improvement in your mood? A feeling of ease or release?

- ° *Mental*: Are thoughts a little quieter?

- ° *Egoic*: A sense of openness or connection?

5. **Acknowledge:** Simply acknowledge whatever you feel (or don't feel) *without* judgement.

Laughter is truly liberating. It's a direct pathway back to joy, presence, and alignment. Remember this simple, powerful tool you always have available.

Now, let's further examine the role of the Mental Body.

CHAPTER 30
TRUST IN THE MENTAL BODY

Beyond logic lies a mind guided by heart, intuition, and trust.

I am fascinated by the Mental Body and its intricate relationship with the brain, intellect, and our overall mindset. A state of trust and alignment in the Mental Body powerfully shapes our overarching mindset, as this body is the lens through which we interpret and engage with life.

The ways in which we habitually perceive, respond to, and approach challenges reflect whether our Mental Body operates primarily from a place of integrated trust (aligned with deeper egoic knowing and core beliefs of Worthiness, Love, and Freedom), or from patterns of limitation and fear (rooted in misaligned beliefs).

Society prioritizes the Mental Body, favoring knowledge, logic, analysis, and achieving goals. We're trained to think our way through life, sometimes even trying to decide logically what should feel good or be "right" for us. The aligned state I speak of flows differently; it arises from letting the wisdom of the heart gently guide the mind, allowing integrated knowing and intuition to emerge. It's where the knowing (Egoic Body), trust (Mental Body), and feeling (Emotional Body) essential for true alignment blend seamlessly with embodied feeling, rather than just mental calculation. Understanding the mindset operating beneath our thoughts is crucial for achieving this alignment, so let's unpack several prevalent mindsets I regularly encounter.

Before we do, it's vital to address a common human tendency: the belief that we should be able to "know" or intellectually understand everything, especially life's biggest challenges and mysteries. I've worked with so many clients who express deep frustration, sometimes even anger—at God, at life, at themselves—because things happen that defy their logical understanding. They might say, "But I try to be such a good person, why is this happening?" This understandable distress often stems from relying solely on the Mental Body for answers it's not equipped to provide.

Our Mental Body, our intellect, is a powerful tool, but it often operates with a linear, cause-and-effect logic—think of it as having a certain processing capacity, like a computer's CPU. Life, The Universe, The Divine, however you conceive of it, operates on an infinitely vaster scale, a "CPU" beyond our mental comprehension. Its "logic" encompasses a mystery we can't fully grasp with our minds alone. When we try to force life's unfolding into the limited framework of our mental understanding, we create more suffering for ourselves.

True peace and authentic trust in the Mental Body arise when it's informed by a deeper "knowing" from the Egoic Body. This isn't an intellectual "knowing" of facts or reasons, but an intuitive sense of connection to a larger meaning, an inherent trust in life's unfolding, even when it's incomprehensible to the mind. When we access this Egoic Body knowing—that deep-seated sense that despite appearances, there is a purpose, a flow, or simply that "it just is" in a way that transcends our need for mental answers—the Mental Body can relax. It can find genuine *trust*, not because it "*knows*" all the answers, but because it's aligned with a deeper wisdom that accepts the mystery. This is where true peace resides: when our intellectual "knowing" doesn't override our body's deeper wisdom, acknowledging that while we don't intellectually know everything, we can intuitively know our wholeness and connection.

Now, let's unpack several prevalent mindsets I regularly encounter.

Overly Positive Mindset: An overly positive mindset refers to an attitude or perspective that focuses on the bright side of life and regularly expects positive outcomes while suppressing or minimizing authentic interpretations. In my opinion, this mindset sometimes risks glossing over authentic expressions of the emotional body in an attempt to force a positive interpretation onto every situation. We are calling this "toxic positivity" nowadays. At times, this sole focus on the positive can become a form of "spiritual bypassing"—using spiritual beliefs or practices to sidestep or avoid difficult emotions and genuine human experiences. Sometimes things aren't positive, or we're not ready for the positive spin. While a positive mindset can be beneficial, I believe an empowered mindset offers a more holistic and authentic approach to life, which I'll discuss further in this section.

Limited Mindset: Widespread in society, this mindset is underscored by assumptions like "I can't," "Be realistic," "Not enough," and "Change is difficult." Often referred to as the "fixed mindset," this perspective restricts adaptability amidst life's ever-changing landscape.

Victim Mindset: This mindset, pervasive in the mainstream lens of media, involves viewing oneself as powerless against external forces, from other individuals to fate, and at times, even The Divine. Social media's emphasis on topics such as "trauma," "toxic relationships," "gaslighting," and "narcissism" can inadvertently bolster this victim mindset. I am not negating the significance or truth of these issues; rather, I aim to show that an excessive or unbalanced focus on them can be disempowering and keep you stuck.

My philosophy centers on human growth and evolution. As life unfolds, we are poised to learn, adapt, and treasure our experiences. A fulfilling life signifies ongoing commitment to growth and innate curiosity.

Thus, the mindsets I advocate for include:

Empowered Mindset: Rather than mere optimism, an empowered mindset embraces the entirety of human experiences. It acknowledges emotions and situations, treating them with honor, love, and respect. There are moments when life doesn't feel positive, when embracing this reality, making peace with all our emotions, is necessary.

Whether it's a period of loss where you need to lean into grief or moments of fear that arise from uncertainty, acknowledging these sentiments is essential. Some of the most impactful moments in my coaching have been recognizing the pain someone is carrying and guiding them to honor, respect, and love where they are. There is nothing more empowering in life than allowing what is to *be*.

Unlimited Mindset: In contrast to limiting beliefs, an unlimited mindset welcomes change as a constant in life. This is a growth and abundance mindset. It operates on the notion that there's enough for everyone and that success and resources are infinite. It understands life's boundless potential and leans into a world filled with expansion, wealth, and happiness. Everything is possible when aligned with truth.

Victor or Creator Mindset: This mindset encourages us to view ourselves as victors or creators instead of victims. It emphasizes the boundless nature of our inner selves. External events typically prompt introspection, driving us inward. By embracing a victor or creator mindset, we welcome life with all its unpredictability, joys, and opportunities. Additionally, we feel empowered to address experiences that might not meet our desires, opting for introspection instead of external blame.

To fortify your mindset, immerse yourself in continuous learning. Knowledge and skill acquisition pave the way for endless joy. The essence of life is embedded in growth and evolution, propelled by ceaseless learning and self-enhancement.

As we've uncovered different mindsets and their implications, we can now explore the nature and characteristics of these mindsets. A mindset that is not connected to the heart reflects logic, rationalization, and analytics. In contrast, a mindset that's integrated with the heart is guided by intuition, knowing, and trust. Similarly, a mindset rooted in limiting viewpoints tends to mirror pain, struggle, and suffering. In contrast, a mindset in line with The Unconditional Three operates at peak strength.

In the subsequent section, we'll see how aligning the Egoic Body can bolster an empowered, unlimited, and victor/creator mindset.

CHAPTER 31
SURRENDER IN THE EGOIC BODY

Integrating surrender into our daily lives entails moving beyond the intellectual concept of "surrender" to truly trusting, feeling, and living its embodied essence.

Throughout this book, I've encouraged leaning on your religious and spiritual convictions to fortify alignment. However, through my professional coaching, I've observed that this suggestion can be a significant source of resistance.

It's important to see that, while commonly used interchangeably, "religious" and "spiritual" can have distinct connotations. Religious beliefs typically refer to a structured system of faith with established doctrines, rituals, and communities. Spiritual beliefs, on the other hand, can be more personal and individualized, drawing on a broader range of practices and perspectives on the meaning of life and connection to something greater than oneself.

Too frequently, individuals, due to their religious upbringing and cultural influences, are instructed on what or how to believe rather than being guided to genuinely feel and connect with their own perspectives.

While the Physical Body might be engaged through practices like charity or fasting, and the Mental Body through prayer or study, resistance often arises from misalignment in the Emotional Body (perhaps feeling numbness, fear, or even anger towards The Divine) and/or the Egoic Body (disconnection or lacking foundational knowing or trust). This misalignment can distort our connection, obstructing the uninhibited flow of genuine spiritual affinity.

As a result, many struggle with self-doubt, fearing that uncertainty implies a lack of genuine faith. It's pivotal to realize that exploring and questioning our beliefs does not equate to a lack of faith. To probe, question, and seek while remaining rooted in your core beliefs is entirely possible.

Mattain Moment 41: **Connecting with Your Inner Truth**

Exploring beliefs can bring up all sorts of feelings, so let's check in.

1. **Awareness**: Take a breath. Bring awareness to your own spiritual or religious beliefs, or perhaps the questions and uncertainties you hold. What *feelings* arise as you consider them right now? Comfort? Doubt? Confusion? Resistance? Peace? Curiosity?

2. **Body Check**: Where do you feel these sensations in your Physical Body? Maybe openness in the chest, vibration in the throat, calmness in the belly, tingling or pressure at your brow (third eye), or a sense of expansion at the crown of your head? Just notice.

3. **Inner Resonance**: Now, set aside any external "shoulds" for a moment. Tune into your own deep inner knowing, perhaps your heart space. Without needing words, what feels true or resonant for you right now about connection or meaning?

4. **Allow**: Acknowledge whatever is present—the beliefs, the doubts, the feelings, the inner resonance—without judgement. They're all part of your unique path.

Your connection to truth is within *you*.

True faith involves honoring our journey, acknowledging a higher power, embracing life's mysteries, and staying receptive to greater truth.

With this approach, you can remain open to investigating the greater meaning while simultaneously staying grounded in truth.

We are naturally curious beings, meant to question and seek. This curiosity does not deem one "blasphemous," but rather reflects our humanity.

Contemplative practices like prayer, meditation, and mindfulness are powerful catalysts for aligning the Egoic Body. In today's rapid-paced world, pausing to be present is invaluable. While meditation and mindfulness have become popular, their essence lies in realizing our profound existence. They sharpen our focus, leading us beyond incessant mental chatter to non-duality (uninhibited connection between oneself and the universe).

As a meditation teacher on Insight Timer, I have the honor of both witnessing and contributing to a platform that provides a wealth of content suited to a variety of preferences and stages of spiritual practice. I encourage you to immerse yourself in this resource and, if you haven't already, follow my teachings there.

Prayer is a beautiful practice of communicating with a higher power. Regardless of religious affiliation, prayer can connect us, bring peace, and enrich presence. When rooted in trust and surrender to a higher power, prayer becomes a powerful act of faith. In such moments of genuine surrender, our desires transition to the unconditional, resting in the knowledge that whatever unfolds is in accordance with the highest good, at a time that is for the highest good. To me, this ideal is the embodiment of beauty and the true essence of life.

The primary intent of meditation is to train the mind's muscles to focus so intensely that it eventually transitions to a state of "un-focus," propelling us from an individual awareness to one of universal interconnectedness, often described as non-duality. Meditation acts as a vehicle permitting the mind to open to new possibilities and connect to something greater than us. By honing this skill, we can more effectively process and express emotions, thoughts, and desires across The Four Bodies, meeting life's challenges with more ease and grace.

Mindfulness is a form of heightened awareness of the present moment. When practicing mindfulness, we observe our thoughts, feelings, sensations, and environment neutrally. We are fully present and engaged in the here and now. Mindfulness can be practiced at any time, whether eating, walking, talking, doing the dishes, or during any other activity.

"But, Manal, I'm bad at meditation!" Dispelling the myth of being "bad" at meditation or mindfulness is vital. Much like breathing, accessing meditative states is natural to our brain. Brainwaves common during meditation and deep relaxation (like theta waves)[39] are actually the dominant state in early childhood.[40] Think of meditation/mindfulness as mental exercise—it's about engagement, practice, and growth. It's not about controlling the mind but about strengthening your ability to focus while also finding comfort in moments of "un-focus."

Some view meditation as unfamiliar or even conflicting with their religious viewpoints. Yet meditation is not an obscure ritual; it is simply a conduit to sync The Four Bodies, bridging physical and spiritual realms. Far from opposing faith, meditation complements it, strengthening our connection with ourselves, life, and life's higher meaning.

With this notion of strengthening our Four Bodies, let's unveil tactics for alignment.

---

[39] Sharp, Loretta Graziano. "Mind Your Theta: Achieving Theta Activity Through Meditation." *Psychology Today*, Sussex Publishers, 24 Jan. 2022, www.psychologytoday.com/us/blog/your-neurology/202201/mind-your-theta-achieving-theta-activity-meditation. Accessed 7 May 2025.
[40] Orekhova, E., Stroganova, T., Posikera, I., & Elam, M. (2006). "EEG theta rhythm in infants and preschool children." *Clinical Neurophysiology, 117*(5), 1047-1062. https://doi.org/10.1016/j.clinph.2005.12.027

CHAPTER 32
GUIDING PRINCIPLES
FOR ALIGNMENT

Presence is more than a state; it's a celebration of the self fully immersed in each moment.

We've identified the power of The Four Bodies and examined how cultivating Acceptance, Compassion, Trust, and Surrender amplifies our ability to harmoniously align our Four Bodies and remain anchored in the present. The following pages detail guiding principles that support arriving at and maintaining harmony. To help you integrate these concepts experientially, you'll find strategically placed Mattain Moments to put each principle into practice right away.

Intention: Setting clear intentions is paramount. Articulate your intentions and desires. This practice can be done quietly to yourself or shared with another. Ensure you state your intentions and desires in the positive, i.e., "I want x, y, z," rather than "I do not want x, y, and z." Once your intentions are clear, the next step is to truly believe them.

Mattain Moment 42: **Establishing Your Intention**

Let's bring this principle to life.

1. Set an intention. For example: "My intention is to reframe anxiety, gain awareness of my fears and physical body expressions, and/or connect with my desires for freedom and inner peace."

2. Imagine this intention unfolding. How does this possibility express in your Physical Body? Notice any subtle responses—perhaps a slight softening in your shoulders, a deeper breath, a warmth in your belly?

3. What sensations arise in your Emotional Body as you hold this intention? Fear? Curiosity? Hope? Openness? Gentleness? Witness these feelings from a place of openness and curiosity.

4. Observe your Mental Body. Are there any judgements or doubts present? Are thoughts calm or busy? Simply notice and allow.

5. Bring awareness to your Egoic Body—your core "I AM" or sense of self. How does this intention land here? Notice if there's an inner nod of alignment, a feeling of "Yes, this resonates with my deeper truth." Also, notice if any subtle resistance or tension arises—perhaps a flicker of familiar fear related to "not being good enough," "not ready yet," "not capable enough," or "not free enough" to embody this intention. Simply acknowledge whatever's present.

6. Breathe into the most resonant, empowering sensation or feeling for a few moments. Anchor this felt sense of your intention within you.

Understanding and anchoring your intention into your body is essential. But what if part of you is still not aligned with that intention? Enter the power of *belief*. Trust, know, and believe you can do it. You can accomplish all that you desire. You. Can. Do. It. With belief firmly in place, focus on what drives your actions: your desires.

Mattain Moment 43: **Cultivating Belief**

Your intention is set. Now, let's set your belief.

1. Recall the anchored feeling of your intention from the last Mattain Moment.

2. Bring the principle of "You. Can. Do. It." into your awareness.

3. Scan your body now. Where does the feeling of belief (or even just "Maybe I can") show up? Is it a subtle strength in your core? A warmth spreading in your chest? An openness across your brow? Find even the smallest flicker.

4. Simultaneously, notice where doubt may feel present (perhaps tightness in the jaw, a knot in the stomach, tension in the neck). Witness it, without judgement.

5. Gently hold awareness of that sensation of doubt or resistance you just noticed. For just a breath or two, simply allow this feeling to fully surface and be present, without needing to push it away, analyze it, or fix it. Just observe, with neutral awareness.

6. Now, consciously bring your focus to and gently breathe into the area where you felt belief or possibility earlier. With each breath, imagine or feel that sensation expanding, becoming a little stronger, warmer, and more solid.

7. Hold this felt sense of "I can," knowing that belief is a muscle we strengthen through practice and awareness.

Desire: Engage in practices driven by a genuine desire rather than out of "need." For tasks that might seem less pleasurable, like laundry or dishes, wait until a genuine desire appears, serving a larger goal such as cleanliness. Instead of focusing on restrictions, unlock your motivation in the broader benefits. For example, frame your approach to nutrition as "I want to be healthy," or "I feel best when I eat well, and I love to feel great," which promote clean eating, rather than "I can't eat this," or "I'm frustrated that I can't eat what I really want." When thinking of work, instead of saying, "I need to work to pay the bills," find the deeper inspiration, acknowledging that work enables you to lead the life you desire. I advocate for even changing the term "work" to "play" or "homework" to "homeplay." As your desires shape your actions, let your inner inspiration be the guiding force.

Trust Your Inspiration: Let your inner inspiration and good intentions guide you to what's best for you. When you hold clarity in what is desired, your inspirations will lead you towards all that harmonizes with your desires. Inspiration begets joy, which brings us to our next principle.

Pleasure: Immerse yourself in activities that genuinely spark joy, passion, and love within you. Life is meant to be enjoyed. Find joy in everything you do. Do things that you love. Enjoy life! This joy should be cherished and celebrated at every step.

Delight in the Journey: Find joy and playfulness not just in every act, but in every step, too. Enjoy the process. Be mindful of not rushing; time is an experience, not just a ticking clock.

Let Go of the Concept of Time: Concentrate on the unfolding of the journey, not just the end goal. Release the constraints of time and unfulfilled expectations and place your trust in life's natural flow. This focus requires a steady and consistent approach.

Consistency: Through regular practice, these activities will seamlessly integrate into your lifestyle. It takes commitment to convert an action into an integrated habit. Enjoy the road towards achieving this consistency.

Celebrate Every Step: Every moment you engage is a step forward. Relish your progress. Celebrate each moment, each breath. As you cherish these moments, maintain a conscious note of them.

Awareness: Regularly take time to reflect on your growth and congruence with your intentions and desires. Self-reflection amplifies your connection to your inner truth and helps you "hear yourself" to adapt to your changing desires.

Mattain Moment 44: **Awareness & Celebrating Progress**

1. Take a moment for Awareness. Gently scan your Four Bodies now. Notice any changes, however small, in your physical sensations, emotional tone, mental clarity, or sense of self since you began this chapter, and perhaps even since you started this book.

2. Recall one insight, feeling, or opening you experienced while reading or during any of these Mattain Moments.

3. Place a hand on your heart space. Take a slow, deep breath.

4. As you exhale, honor yourself for showing up, for being willing to take these steps.

5. What does this act of self-acknowledgement and celebration feel like in your body? Notice any warmth, softness, gratitude, or quiet pride.

6. Savor the beauty of this moment.

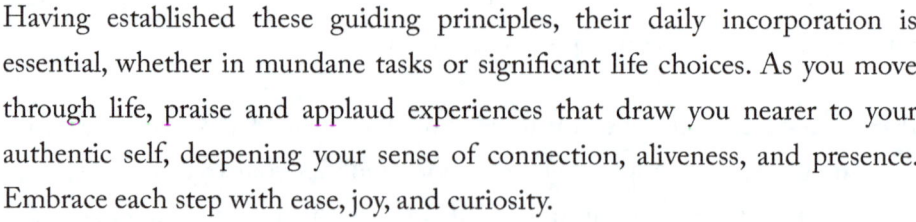

Having established these guiding principles, their daily incorporation is essential, whether in mundane tasks or significant life choices. As you move through life, praise and applaud experiences that draw you nearer to your authentic self, deepening your sense of connection, aliveness, and presence. Embrace each step with ease, joy, and curiosity.

As previously mentioned, redefine every choice and action as an extension of your true inspirations and desires, always keeping your highest motivations at the forefront.

In the next chapter, we'll introduce methods to measure and celebrate your growth, allowing you to continuously refine your approach. You'll gain further clarity as you implement these ideas as blueprints for a fulfilling life.

CHAPTER 33
MASTERY IN ALIGNMENT

Every step we take in life, whether forward or perceived "backward," is a dance of learning, evolving, and growing.

The pursuit of unconditional Worthiness, Love, and Freedom is a never-ending practice of continuous growth and expansion. It's a path along which you develop the muscles of Acceptance, Compassion, Trust, and Surrender. I've worked with many clients, friends, and seekers who are frustrated because they feel like "they've already dealt with that"—that abandonment, that loneliness, that sadness, that feeling of unworthiness. But remember, aligning with our infinite nature is a lifelong pursuit.

Let's consider a simple analogy: Would a single cup of coffee or one small square of chocolate satisfy you for life? Would a singular bicep curl alter your physique? The answer is no. These actions are experiences we enjoy and efforts we undertake repeatedly; each instance brings a new sense of satisfaction and progress.

Similarly, aligning with new beliefs, thoughts, emotions, and physical manifestations is an ongoing process. Just as physical fitness requires consistent effort, spiritual growth is an evolution of continuous unfolding, which could be visualized as climbing an upward spiral. With each rotation, we revisit familiar territory—old patterns, beliefs, and challenges—from a higher vantage point, with greater awareness and a wider perspective.

Life continually provides us with feedback and opportunities for growth. Each moment, each encounter, each instant of introspection is a chance to exercise our Egoic, Mental, Emotional, and Physical muscles, symbolizing the thrill and beauty of the human experience.

As we addressed in Part I, societal conditioning and our pasts often lead to limiting beliefs, repressed emotions, and physical pain that can block our growth. These expressions can show up as fears, anxieties, and self-doubts, hindering our alignment. Awareness of these obstacles is the first step towards overcoming them.

Remember that it took a lifetime to adopt these limiting beliefs and patterns. Naturally, it will take time—precisely the time that's right for you—to develop the muscles of unconditional Worthiness, Love, and Freedom.

Given that this development takes time, our approach becomes one of consciously *embracing this unfolding*. This objective involves valuing intention, commitment, focus, and continual growth, while also having fun with the process, treasuring the journey, and celebrating each step.

Mattain Moment 45: **A Moment of Alignment**

Place a hand on your heart. Take one slow, conscious breath in, feeling the simple aliveness within you right now. Hold at the very top of your inhale for just a second. Indulge in this pause—the gap, that silent space of pure wholeness and infinite truth within you. Then, as you slowly breathe out, allow the feeling of stillness and truth from the gap to settle and integrate deeply within your body.

Feel the warmth under your hand—a simple celebration of your presence, your alignment, your aliveness, and your connection to your inner power.

Most importantly, this calibration towards The Unconditional Three is a deeply connected aspect of this amazing unfolding of life. We are part of a collective human experience, united by our shared pursuit of Worthiness, Love, and Freedom. As we cultivate these qualities within ourselves, we also contribute to a more compassionate and loving world.

CHAPTER 34
CELEBRATING YOUR ALIGNMENT

Growth is not merely about reaching a destination, but about navigating the intricate nexus of frequency, duration, and intensity in our experiences.

As we calibrate to The Unconditional Three—Worthiness, Love, and Freedom—it's vital to have a way to measure our progress. This process is not about the total absence of resistance in The Four Bodies—such as misbeliefs, thoughts, emotions, and physical sensations—but a decrease in its *frequency*, *duration*, and *intensity*.

Consider resistant thoughts and emotions. As you progress, you may find they occur less *frequently*. The *duration*, or time spent dwelling on these thoughts or in these emotional states, may decrease. The *intensity*, or power these thoughts and emotions hold over you, may diminish.

Conversely, when it comes to empowering beliefs—those moments of Worthiness, Love, and Freedom—you'll likely notice an increase in their *frequency*. The *duration* of these feelings may extend, filling more of your day-to-day life, and their *intensity* may grow and deepen, leading to stronger experiences of personal power. You may begin to encounter more and more periods of pure contentment with the moment, irrespective of what you may be doing.

I must reiterate that the goal isn't to eliminate all resistant beliefs, thoughts, emotions, or physical discomforts; doing so would render us non-human. These elements are fundamental to our humanness and will be our companions throughout life. Instead of seeking their total eradication, our aim is to recalibrate our internal equilibrium so that *empowering feelings predominate over disempowering ones.* Even in moments of perceived setback or frustration, with heightened awareness, we can gracefully pivot towards Acceptance, Compassion, and Trust. This essence is true growth.

With intention, focus, and commitment, we can shift the balance. We can reach a place where we feel unconditionally empowered, regardless of external circumstances. And eventually, we can perceive all feelings as empowering, no matter their traditional positive or negative labels.

Finally, we surrender. This level of unconditional acceptance is a testament to our growth and a key marker of our movement towards Worthiness, Love, and Freedom.

Importantly, this process is not about labeling feelings as positive or negative, because all feelings serve a purpose. Remember, "It just is." Surrender is the act of using all of life's unfolding to propel you towards Acceptance, Compassion, and Trust.

This reframing is a powerful channel to calibrate to The Unconditional Three.

Mattain Moment 46: **Celebrating Your Growth & Alignment**

Before moving into action, let's take a moment to connect inward and honor ourselves right now.

Take three deep breaths, and with each cycle, don't forget to gently indulge in the gap—that silent space of infinite truth at the top of your inhale and bottom of your exhale.

With each breath out, simply allow yourself to *be*, moving deeper into your own truth.

1. Reflect: Can you recall a recent instance where resistance (a challenging thought, emotion, or sensation) felt less intense, didn't last as long, or didn't appear as frequently as it might have before?

2. Where have you recently noticed a deeper *taste* of embodying Worthiness, Love, or Freedom? Recall moments where this truth felt more palpable, integrated, and present in your core being—perhaps showing up more frequently, lasting longer, or simply feeling more *real* and accessible, even subtly?

3. Acknowledge any small movement, increased awareness, or moment of choosing Acceptance, Compassion, or Trust. Hold yourself in awareness, noticing any feeling (tingling, warmth, or ease) that arises.

4. Allow these sensations to flow in your heart and throughout your body. This ongoing process of awareness, acceptance, and recalibration is the beautiful dance of alignment. Honor yourself, exactly where you are right now.

As you continue reading, get ready to feel the difference. The next section moves beyond mere concepts into action, with case studies and practical strategies designed to help you further embody, understand, and grow.

Celebrate your growth!

Celebrate your expansion!

Celebrate your alignment!

Celebrate your humanness!

SECTION V:
CASE STUDIES: FROM FEAR
TO FREEDOM

Within each of us lies the capacity to transform anxiety, revealing our truest essence of infinite Worthiness, Love, and Freedom.

CHAPTER 35
REAL LIVES, REAL FREEDOM

Beyond every fear lies the possibility for freedom.

As we near the end of this book, we'll dive into real-life stories of individuals who've traveled from fear to freedom. We'll encounter Karina, Alexa, Tony, and Kevin, each with their own unique narrative. These stories aren't just about overcoming obstacles; they're about radical transformation. They're about the evolution from a state of anxiety, rooted in suppressed fears, to a state of freedom, founded on irrefutable worthiness and the pursuit of happiness. Each story illustrates the acts of identifying and acknowledging fears, thereby releasing the grip of anxiety and catalyzing remarkable growth. The insights shared demonstrate the power within each of us to mold anxiety into freedom, fear into courage, and self-doubt into self-worth.

As we absorb ourselves in these stories, we'll see the power of releasing anxiety by acknowledging and allowing underlying fears. The following transformations show that, through the philosophies shared in this book, inviting a lasting state of Worthiness, Love, and Freedom can be *easy*.

I invite you to reflect on your own experience with what we formally called "anxiety" and consider the potential for evolution that lies within you. Use these narratives as sources of inspiration to guide you on your trajectory towards personal growth and freedom.

CHAPTER 36
KARINA'S PROGRESSION

In the midst of our deepest uncertainties, we find our most profound transformations.

Amidst the turbulence of a challenging divorce, Karina found herself enveloped in anxiety and struggling with the overwhelming uncertainty of her future. The practicalities—where to live, the future of her son, managing her finances—were not all that haunted her, but an unfamiliar, pervasive unease stemming from a place deep within. Her story, unfolding from this point, is not just personal. Her transformation serves as living proof of the energy of The Mattain Five-Step Process, a vivid application of its concepts, an investigation into the expressions of The Four Bodies, and a deep dive into the impact of conditioning.

My investigation with Karina started with awareness. Karina opened herself up, observing her looping mind and physical discomfort. She was constantly stressed, her body was tense, her thoughts compulsive and disruptive; overall, she felt extremely uncomfortable. When guided to become attentive to her emotions, she encountered an overwhelming surge of fear and sadness.

Through tapping into her emotions, Karina experienced a moment of vulnerability, breaking down, crying, and confessing, "I am not sure how I'm going to do this. I can't do this. I am such a failure." But this was more than a breakdown; it was a break*through*.

By exposing the misbeliefs nestled within her Egoic Body, Karina sparked an emotional release that showcased a pivotal truth about her self-worth.

Upon further exploration, it became clear that Karina's sense of worthiness had been intricately tethered to maintaining a traditional family structure. This concept was rooted in the setting in which she was raised, where being unmarried or undergoing a divorce was deemed a failure. This sense of failure and accompanying feelings of unworthiness it bred were not innately hers, but conditioned responses from her upbringing.

Karina achieved a crucial stage of awareness regarding her Four Bodies, clearly discerning the expressions of her physical symptoms, repressed emotions, mental narratives, and misbeliefs originating from her conditioning. The recognition of this conditioning—how it shaped her misbeliefs and expressions across her Four Bodies—marked a turning point in her development of self-awareness.

This pivotal realization illustrated Step 1—Awareness—of The Mattain Five-Step Process. Now, Karina was poised to comprehend how the external unfolding of life was signaling her internal desires.

Karina's admission of feeling like a failure unveiled a longing for worthiness, signifying her transition into Step 2: Acknowledgement. This Acknowledgement led her to center her attention, and therefore her energy, on her true desires, facilitating a redirection away from the undesired.

This epiphany was truly the climax of the moment: the actualization that Karina was not only mourning her divorce, but a lack of trust in her own worth. The beauty of The Mattain Method lies in the liberation that begins upon seeing authentic expressions of self.

Karina began to see her situation in a new light, indicating Step 3: Appreciation. This reframe aided her in confronting her fears related to control and freedom, leading her to adopt an "I'm doing the best I can" mindset. Her newfound intellectual clarity fostered emotional openness and gratitude, enabling her to authentically appreciate her current position and the road that led her there. As she became aware of her resistance to her situation, she found acceptance for her present circumstances and her progression thus far.

Karina's tears during her initial release, brought on by perceiving her suppressed sadness and "sense of failure," signaled an unconscious relinquishment of held resistance. Taking a deep, conscious breath, she opened to a second release, now with the awareness of acceptance. She was able to intellectually perceive how she was tying her worthiness to external conditioning instead of recognizing her unconditional worthiness simply by virtue of being human. This realization marked Step 4: Allowing. In this instance, it was Karina's capacity to stay present with this understanding and any feelings that arose with it—perhaps sadness for past struggles, guilt over her perceived failures, or fear about the future—without pushing them away. She let the realization settle, making space for the discomfort of seeing her old patterns, thereby releasing her resistance to this deeper awareness.

Discovering her inherent Worthiness and confronting fears around control and freedom enabled Karina to recalibrate her life, fostering a deeper level of happiness. The key to her liberation was seeing her resistance. The restrictive shell in which she had confined herself began to crack. Karina began to see a Worthiness and Freedom in simply being herself, unbound by the external constructs of wife and family. She yielded to her present reality, demonstrating Step 5: Surrender.

Karina's progression from suffocating anxiety to self-acceptance illustrates the potency of The Mattain Five-Step Process and related methodologies. Through Awareness, Acknowledgement, Appreciation, Allowing, and Surrender, she reconciled her internal and external worlds, reshaping both by confronting and deconstructing embedded narratives and misbeliefs. Her story illuminates the revolutionary power of these approaches, providing a tangible narrative of evolving from tormenting turmoil to true tranquility.

CHAPTER 37
ALEXA'S REFLECTION

True perfection is recognizing that all facets of self, even those we deem imperfections, are inherently perfect.

Caught in the throes of perfectionism and worry, Alexa meticulously orchestrated every aspect of her life, from arranging the smallest details of her day to organizing gatherings and managing social events. Striving to execute every task flawlessly, she held a desire to meet external expectations which propelled her into a constant state of distress. A simple set of instructions could send her spiraling into overwhelm, proof of the relentless pressure she put on herself. Despite being the go-to person for parties and events, her internal cost was steep, leading to perpetual stress, fatigue, and anxiety. By the time she came to me, not only was she exhausted, but her family was also bearing the brunt of her emotional distress.

As Alexa and I initiated our work together, she began to feel the interplay of her Four Bodies, starting with her narrative, an expression of the stories held within her Mental Body. Alexa expressed that she felt as though she had to do everything for everybody, and not just do it, but do it perfectly. She conveyed a feeling of not being free to do what she wanted; she felt obligated to meet everyone else's expectations. Despite all her efforts, she never felt good enough. She was never able to relax, always looking ahead to the next deadline, appointment, or task. Layered atop was a guilt, a misbelief that she "should be happy" with her seemingly good life, further complicating her emotional landscape.

I encouraged Alexa to dig deeper into her emotional state. I had noticed a discrepancy between her frequent use of "I feel" and the lack of expressed emotions in our dialogues, so I gently pointed this out to her. As she peered inward, Alexa discovered a well of fatigue and frustration; with further investigation, a sadness tinged with anger emerged. She confessed that, at times, a flash of anger would unexpectedly surface, revealing itself to those around her.

By Deconstructing the Key Lime Pie to identify the expressions of her distinct Bodies, Alexa had the following breakthroughs:

- **Mental Body:** Her mind was regularly scattered with limiting thoughts and a victim mentality, particularly evident when she insisted she was catering to everyone else's needs.

- **Physical Body:** Alexa's fatigue was a tangible indication of the considerable stress and tension she was experiencing. This physical state mirrored the resistance present in all her Four Bodies due to misalignment from her own personal desires and her authentic self.

- **Emotional Body:** We observed that Alexa was "PAINS-ing" her emotions.

  ○ *Projecting:* She attributed her lack of freedom to others.

  ○ *Amplifying:* Her anger would rapidly intensify, targeting those nearby.

  ○ *Intellectualizing:* She rationalized her emotions, thinking she "should be happy."

  ○ *Negating:* She denied her anger.

  ○ *Suppressing:* She held back her frustration, sadness, and happiness.

- **Egoic Body:** Although Alexa expressed a feeling of not feeling free, not feeling good enough, and sadness, these expressions reflected her deeper egoic beliefs of a lack of worthiness, happiness, and freedom.

Armed with these insights, we sought the origins of Alexa's misbeliefs. We uncovered that, during her upbringing, Alexa was conditioned to constantly seek parental approval. Cast in the role of the "good girl," she was taught to prioritize others' needs and chase perfection while neglecting her desires. Her worth was defined by her "doing" and external validation, rather than her being.

This revelation provided a substantial amount of "data" for Step 1: Awareness.

Step 2: Acknowledgement naturally followed the process of Deconstructing the Key Lime Pie. Through examining Alexa's narrative, we uncovered a projection of her own perceived lack of Worthiness, Love/happiness, and Freedom. This clarity illuminated her realization: "Ah, I understand now, I desire Worthiness, Love/happiness, and Freedom." She began to feel lighter simply by moving her focus to her desires, rather than dwelling on the unwanted.

We were poised to quickly move to Step 3: Appreciation. Alexa found that her need for control and perfectionism reflected her inner yearning for freedom. She felt compelled to do what others wanted rather than follow her own desires. But she prioritized others' needs before her own, attempting to fill her worthiness bucket through external validation. When she began saying "no" to certain activities, she discovered that others were accommodating, and that she possessed more freedom than she'd initially perceived. By tapping into her inner self to guide her desires, Alexa naturally began to feel a stronger trust in herself. She began to understand that true worthiness wasn't earned through others' validation but cultivated through self-acceptance and authentic living. Each act of trusting her inner guidance and valuing her own desires calibrated her to her internal inherent worth, independent of external feedback. This growing trust enhanced her sense of freedom and broke the cycle of feeling controlled and confined.

Alexa also noticed that her happiness was forced, anchored in thoughts like, "I have everything; I should be thankful." Taking a step back, she found that she wasn't fully allowing herself to express feelings of frustration and fatigue. When she let go of the "should" and allowed the natural expressions of her Emotional Body with compassion, she found that acknowledging her frustration and tiredness led to internal satisfaction and peace.

Alexa didn't demonstrate a dramatic Step 4: Allowing. However, her release was evident in the subconscious manner through which she could intellectually "see" the relationship between her Four Bodies. Through her awareness of her desires, and a recognition of trust in the human experience, she began to allow the resistance within her Four Bodies to soften and dissipate naturally, leading to alignment. She established an intention to master a sense of Acceptance, Compassion, and Trust to guide her Four Bodies into a perpetual state of Surrender, Step 5.

Through applying The Mattain Five Steps, Alexa sculpted a road to her completeness. Her engagement with Deconstructing the Key Lime Pie revealed enlightening insights, particularly her meticulous management of emotions, vividly evidenced by how she "PAINS-ed" her Emotional Body.

The stories of Alexa and Karina exemplify how the proactive application of awareness and intentional self-discovery can guide us towards The Unconditional Three. While everyone's course to harmony and authentic expression of truth is deeply personal, these narratives illustrate that the terrain can be navigated with clear and deliberate intention, shedding light on the universality of our emotional and human experiences.

CHAPTER 38
TONY'S TRANSFORMATION

Awareness is the first step towards transformation. In understanding our anxieties, we begin to see the path to inner peace.

Tony's inner narrative was dominated by sentiments like "I feel anxiety," "I am anxious," "Life is so difficult," and "Life is a struggle."

As we started our sessions together, we began by inventorying these manifestations through Deconstructing the Key Lime Pie. We dissected the dynamics across Tony's Four Bodies: Mental, Physical, Emotional, and Egoic. His mind was awash with obsessive thoughts, looping endlessly, and his Physical Body mirrored this unrest. His jaw remained tense, his shoulders tightened, his heart raced, and his head felt unbearably heavy.

Like Alexa, Tony initially found it challenging to articulate his emotions, largely resorting to broad descriptors such as feeling "overwhelmed" or "not good enough." It's common, especially early in the course of first developing self-awareness, to believe you are echoing the Emotional Body, when in fact you are merely regurgitating the mind's narrative. I encouraged Tony to probe beyond these superficial thoughts and genuinely engage with his emotions, particularly his unacknowledged fears.

Gradually, Tony was able to tap into his emotions, uncovering fears related to financial inadequacy: the apprehension of not having enough money, being unable to pay bills or manage credit card debt, and a pervasive dread of relentless financial demands. A scarcity of money and consequent lack of security incited feelings of frustration.

As Tony connected deeper into these fears, a spectrum of emotions surfaced: fear, sadness, and anger. Once he allowed himself to recognize these emotions, the floodgates of his Egoic misbeliefs opened. He confessed feelings of insufficiency and incapability, of being unworthy and trapped. Tony unveiled the concealed misbeliefs within his Egoic Body through a "dance of awareness" across The Four Bodies.

Tony then had a watershed moment. He had buried these fears, never confronting his core conviction of feeling "not good enough." He had an epiphany: "It's not just about the money," he realized. "It's how I perceive myself. If I feel unworthy, no amount of money will ever suffice."

He came to see that his external financial woes mirrored his internal strife. His dwindling bank account and mounting credit card debt starkly showcased his feelings of unworthiness and perceived lack of control and freedom. His external experience was a beacon, guiding him to confront his internal struggles. This process marked a potent unfolding of Step 1: Awareness, positioning Tony to identify his hidden desires.

At this point, transitioning to Step 2: Acknowledgement became straightforward. Tony's desires were transparent: he yearned for a sense of worthiness and a state of freedom. Additionally, he determined that he was harboring a misbelief that happiness would materialize once his financial situation improved, mistakenly attributing happiness to external circumstances rather than recognizing it as an internal state of being.

Tony was astonished to see how his relationships with money and security were directly aligned with The Unconditional Three.

Moving onto Step 3: Appreciation was also easy for Tony. He'd been following my teachings for some time and appreciated the beauty of the human experience. He naturally exuded Acceptance, Compassion, and Trust for himself and his life's unfolding. But now, he had revelations into where to direct these qualities to facilitate alignment with The Unconditional Three.

In Step 4: Allowing, Tony revisited his watershed moment from Step 1. Instead of just intellectually understanding his past release, he focused on any lingering resistance or fear sensations still present in his Four Bodies. He practiced consciously allowing these feelings and thoughts to be without fighting them or needing them to change, recognizing that his suffering stemmed more from resisting these inner experiences than from the experiences themselves. He breathed into the discomfort, creating space.

Then, moving into Step 5: Surrender, building on this non-resistance, Tony consciously focused on aligning his desires with the truth of his innate Worthiness, Love, and Freedom. By deeply Accepting his present reality, fostering Compassion for his journey, and Trusting the larger flow of life (embodying ACT), the need to negate his old fears lessened. He described moving into a state of profound ease and acceptance of "what is." The process of moving from fear towards these truths became progressively lighter and more accessible for him.

Tony's transformation represents a remarkable evolution from anxiety to awareness. His initial narrative, saturated with stress and a perpetual echo of "not good enough," evolved into a conscious acknowledgement of his fears and intentional synchronicity with The Unconditional Three. By attentively interpreting the patterns within his Four Bodies, Tony not only rewrote his internal narrative, but also altered his external reality.

Tony's progression from a state of constant anxiety and struggle to a newfound awareness of his fears represents the power of direct observation and the embracing of Acceptance, Compassion, and Trust. This development not only brought Tony a sense of satisfaction but also unveiled a depth of fulfillment that had long eluded him, further illustrating that the path from anxiety to freedom is navigated through the conscious allowing of our fears.

CHAPTER 39
KEVIN'S SHIFT

Labels are but words. Our emotions and experiences define our true essence.

Kevin's story began with a label, a diagnosis that made him feel out of control. He was diagnosed with psychosis, which came with obsessive thoughts and a belief that his medical condition controlled him. Despite deep spiritual connections, his "human self" felt overwhelmed by his diagnosis, prompting us to focus on his Emotional Body.

Upon beginning our work, Kevin discovered that his initial unwillingness to understand and acknowledge his emotions fueled his looping thoughts. He developed an intellectual awareness of the value of his emotional feedback system and began to willingly acknowledge his feelings. He recognized that, alongside the label of "psychosis," his inability to witness his emotions kept him disconnected from his body.

At first, Kevin would describe his feelings as thoughts, such as "I am not good enough" or "I am not as good as others." However, these were not feelings, but misbeliefs steeped in limiting thoughts and a victim mentality. Gradually, Kevin was able to awaken to the feelings underlying these conceptions.

He initially met his newfound relationship with his emotions with unease, which gradually morphed into curiosity. Slowly, he began to appreciate his ability to feel. He scanned through his body, attempting to observe the sentiments of his Emotional Body.

A pivotal moment arrived when Kevin pinpointed that underneath his sentiments of "not good enough" lay actual feelings of fear, anger, and sadness.

Acknowledging these feelings marked a celebratory breakthrough. He identified the sensations materializing in his Emotional Body.

Following this breakthrough, Kevin found it easier to perceive his emotions for what they were, rather than labeling them as products of his mind or psychosis. He began allowing his emotions to guide him towards uninhibited Worthiness, Love, and Freedom.

Kevin's story is a testament to the radical power of acknowledging and being with emotions. It illustrates his growth from resistance to acceptance, and a significant breakthrough in allowing his emotions. This shift not only depicts Kevin's progression of his relationship with his emotions but also showcases that overcoming labels and embracing our feelings can guide us towards greater self-growth and acceptance.

Do you see a pattern in all our case studies? This pattern is not unique to Karina, Alexa, Tony, or Kevin. As a society, we've turned off our capacity to tune into our Emotional Bodies. It's time to reclaim power over our emotional feedback systems. Let's examine common patterns at both the societal and individual levels.

CHAPTER 40
KEY INSIGHTS FROM CASE STUDIES

From each story of struggle emerges patterns of strength, lessons of empowerment, and the shared human experience of seeking freedom.

As we reflect on these powerful anecdotes, we see several themes and key points that can guide us in moving from fear to Worthiness, Love, and Freedom. Here are some main takeaways:

Awareness: Through awareness, we objectively bring the expressions of our Four Bodies into clearer focus. This involves objectively observing the prominent ways these Bodies manifest and setting a deliberate intention to acknowledge these expressions with effusive acceptance.

Acknowledging and Confronting Fears: The subsequent step involves acknowledging our fears to alleviate the anxieties they generate. This is a deliberate action in the process of overcoming them.

Exploring Limiting Thoughts and Beliefs: Our thoughts and beliefs can greatly influence our experiences of fear and anxiety. By challenging these patterns, we start to expand our perspectives and open to new possibilities.

Transitioning from the Undesired to the Desired: The "a-ha" moment truly blossoms when we shift our focus from what we don't want to what we earnestly desire.

Embracing Self-Worth: Awakening to our worthiness is a key aspect of transcending fear. When we appreciate that we are worthy simply because we exist, we can let go of fears related to inadequacy or failure.

Experiencing Unconditional Happiness: I urge you to own that happiness is not tied to external conditions or circumstances—it is an internal state we can choose at any moment. By embracing unconditional happiness, we can rise above fear and anxiety as we realize that our inner state of joy is not dependent on external events or outcomes.

Finding Freedom: Freedom is not just about overcoming fear; it's about recognizing our inherent truth and natural capacity to live authentically, releasing the need to control. When we reframe internal beliefs and release identification with societal expectations that no longer serve us, we uncover the freedom already within, opening to joy and fulfillment.

The Power of ACT: Expressing Acceptance, Compassion, and Trust towards ourselves, consciously or unconsciously, serves as a conduit to shaping fears. These human expressions naturally counter our fears, facilitating a movement from resistance to allowing.

To bring our time together in these pages to a close, we'll focus on integrating these truths and celebrating the aligned life now within your reach. Each step has been a testament to the power of self-awareness, Acceptance, Compassion, Trust, Surrender, and the determination to grow beyond fear and achieve a life of Worthiness, Love, and Freedom. As we conclude, may the clarity you've gained from these pages light your way as you continue to choose awareness, to choose freedom, to choose your authentic self.

REFLECTIONS ON PART II: FROM FEAR TO FREEDOM

We sought to know, dared to trust, opened to feel. Now, in the stillness of being, freedom simply is.

As we draw the curtain on Part II: From Fear to Freedom, I find myself reflecting on the incredible adventure we've taken together. Through these pages, we've dug deep, seeking to transcend our fears, not by pushing them aside, but by deciphering their messages and transmuting their energy.

Throughout these sections, we've shined a light on The Universal Fears. Recognizing these fears deepened our self-awareness and fostered a sense of shared humanity, reminding us that we are not alone. In this collective realization, we found an opportunity to connect, grow, and thrive. Let's review:

- **Fear of Failure:** This fear manifests as feelings of unworthiness and a fear of not being good enough. The antidote is Acceptance, recognizing and affirming our inherent *Worthiness*. It's powerful to ascertain that perfection isn't a state to be achieved; rather, we embody perfection through our core nature.

- **Fear of Not Being Loved:** This fear arises from our longing for happiness. Compassion is the antidote to this fear, guiding us towards embracing our inner *Love*.

- **Fear of Death:** Our fear of uncertainty or control often translates into a fear of death. Trust serves as an antidote to this fear, aligning with infinite *Freedom*.

The Universal Fears represent our disconnection from The Unconditional Three: Worthiness, Love, and Freedom.

We've uncovered these antidotes through the power of ACT: Acceptance, Compassion, and Trust. Through Acceptance, we nurture a sincere sense of self-worth; with Compassion, we fill our Emotional Body, cultivating love within and around; and through Trust, we confront life's uncertainties, embracing a boundless sense of freedom.

The ultimate manifestation of ACT leads us to Surrender, or in Mattain-Speak, ACTS: a state where resistance dissolves and we attune to life's natural rhythm. In ACTS, our Four Bodies achieve complete harmony and alignment.

Having grasped the nature of our fears and their antidotes, a structured approach is essential for calibrating them towards empowerment. The Mattain Five-Step Process offers this guidance, molding our relationship with fear into actionable steps towards freedom. This systematic method leads us from realizing resistance to embracing surrender, ensuring we remain present and aligned with our Four Bodies, thereby cultivating a life of boundless potential.

Step 1: Awareness: We become attuned to the fears and other resistance within our Four Bodies. Through Deconstructing the Key Lime Pie, we objectively observe the expressions of our Four Bodies, recognizing friction as an indication of what is undesired.

Step 2: Acknowledgement: Next, we build upon Awareness. By determining what is undesired, we gain clarity on what is desired. Here is where we transmute our awareness of resistance into The Unconditional Three.

Step 3: Appreciation: I typically think of the third step as a bridge— one that connects the Acknowledgement of our fears to their evolution.

Through ACT, we realize that our fears are not barriers but pathways, guiding lights directing us towards The Unconditional Three: Worthiness, Love, and Freedom.

Step 4: Allowing: After Appreciation (Step 3), we permit the expressions in our Four Bodies (identified in Step 1) to be present without resistance or judgment. This non-resistance dissolves the suffering tied to fighting reality and opens the door to deeper alignment and ease.

Step 5: Surrender: Our journey culminates in the state of Surrender: full alignment where we embrace ACT and life in its infinite entirety.

In essence, the process of Transcending Fears serves as our compass. We find that once understood and reshaped, *fear becomes an ally*, guiding us towards growth and The Unconditional Three. Together, we evolve from reacting to our fears to mastering them, decoding their deeper messages.

The Mattain Five-Step Process serves as a direct route to anchoring firmly in the beauty and power of the present. We now possess the tools to not only become present, but to stay rooted in the now, fully surrender to life, and harmoniously align our Four Bodies.

We concluded with Alchemy for Alignment, where we detailed strategies to strengthen the muscles of our Four Bodies, enabling us to inhabit a state of Surrender more powerfully and consistently. We outlined specific ways and practices to cultivate ACTS within The Four Bodies.

Life is a beautiful opportunity for continuous growth. As we wrap up, let's recognize that calibration to truth is an ongoing process. Every step forward signifies progress in our collective human endeavor as we all strive for congruence with unconditional Worthiness, Love, and Freedom.

The power of Awareness, Acceptance, Compassion, Trust, and Surrender has been evident through each step of our exploration, guiding us to move past fear and evoke a life enriched with beauty. Let's hold onto these insights, allowing them to illuminate the way as we strive to radiate truth and elevate our lives.

CONCLUSION:
THE JOURNEY AHEAD

In every fear lies an opportunity to transcend and find our true essence. Embrace, understand, surrender.

Thank you, from the depths of my heart, for accompanying me on this voyage of self-discovery. Every page turned, every line read, has been a step towards awareness, acceptance, and growth. If you've reached this point (unless, of course, you've jumped ahead—in which case, I still honor your approach!), I trust this expedition has offered you valuable insights, tools, and perspectives.

I also trust I have fulfilled the promise of *Transcending Anxiety: From Fear to Freedom*. In Chapter 8: Shifting the Narrative, we transcended anxiety by aligning our Four Bodies and refining our perception of life from one of struggle, pain, and suffering to one of flow, ease, and allowing. In Chapter 22: Applying The Mattain Five Steps, we harnessed The Mattain Five-Step Process, transforming our fears into roads to freedom. These systems offer enduring strategies to continually guide us towards the lives we aspire to.

Several key takeaways have crystallized over the course of this book:

Anxiety Is a Construct: We began by challenging the conventional perception of "anxiety." Instead of a stifling label, we approached it as an invitation to dig deeper, to see our unacknowledged fears of the future with clarity, and to address them head-on. Through this construct, we transcend anxiety.

The Universality of Fear: Every human inevitably experiences variations of three core fears: the fear of failure, the fear of being unlovable, and the fear of death. These Universal Fears attest to our natural human yearnings for Worthiness, Love, and Freedom. I aspire to instill a sense of empowerment and unity within you by illuminating these fears. Know that you are not flawed or isolated; these fears represent shared facets of human existence and are channels for elevation.

The Unconditional Three: Every manifestation of anxiety or fear becomes a mirror, reflecting an opportunity to recalibrate and align with our intrinsic human pull towards Worthiness, Love, and Freedom—ultimately propelling us towards genuine fulfillment and self-realization.

The Mattain Five-Step Process: This dynamic system is our compass, guiding us to see, understand, and transform our fears into catalysts for actualizing our most profound desires.

The Power of Presence: We culminated our enrichment by embracing the present moment, allowing its unmatched potential to offer joy, peace, and connection.

I genuinely hope this book serves as a source of inspiration, that it reassures you of your worth, brilliance, and capability. That you recognize you're not just normal—you're extraordinary.

This book's message is one of beauty and empowerment. It's about rising above not just anxiety and fear, but any pain or challenge, aligning ourselves with The Unconditional Three: Worthiness, Love, and Freedom.

So, where do you go from here? As I've emphasized throughout, aligning with The Unconditional Three is a lifelong pursuit. I am here for you. If you need motivation, support, or encouragement, be sure to check out my podcast *Attain the Life that You Desire* on Apple Podcasts, Spotify, or YouTube.

Our life evolution unfolds as we embrace our authentic truth, trust it, feel its resonance, and embody it fully. I trust that your curiosity has been sparked.

Yet we have so much more to unpack and learn together. You don't have to do this alone.

I would love to guide you further by inviting you to visit my website: **www. mattain.com**

Here, you can access resources like meditations, talks, and live events. You can connect with me directly at: **www.mattain.com/connect** I'd love to hear from you.

One parting request: If this experience truly helped you transcend anxiety and advance from fear to freedom, I'd be incredibly grateful for your support. A review on Amazon/Goodreads not only amplifies my inspiration as an author but also reassures others that they're not alone. With just a few words, you could guide someone else towards liberation. This cycle is beautiful: You found relief, and now you're helping others find theirs, aiding in my growth as well. Thank you for being part of this collective transformation.

As we part ways for now, remember: Life is ever-evolving, ever-unfolding. Approach it with love, courage, and a sense of wonder. Until our paths cross again, treasure every moment, every experience, and every lesson.

Thank you for allowing me to be a part of your journey.

ACKNOWLEDGEMENTS

This book has emerged from a lifelong knowing; I've always known I would become an author. Developed through the unwavering support and boundless love of many, it stands as a testament to my journey. My family, friends, clients, followers, colleagues, my people: You have all been my sanctuary and my strength.

To my parents, who laid the foundation for me from the very beginning: Your love and wisdom have consistently directed me and shaped my path. I am me, because of you. Thank you, Mom and Dad. I love you both incredibly.

To my siblings, both by birth and by the bond of marriage: You've ventured alongside me, learning, growing, expanding, and evolving; it has been a ride! Thank you, Aiman, Waleed, Nader, and Enjy.

To my babes, Salma, Nisma, and Yusef: You've taught me the importance of honoring each step of the unfolding of life, the depth of unconditional acceptance and love, and the grace of surrender. Through you, I've learned to stop looking to the future and start living in the now. You have always been, and always will be, a significant source of my strength. I love you.

To my nieces and nephews, Aya, Reem, Yasmeen, Zane, Leena, Mila, and Zach: Each of you holds a special place in my heart. Witnessing your growth, your unique expressions, and the paths you're carving has added such beauty, depth, richness, and fun to my life. Love you wholly!

To my grandniece, Nala, the beacon of a new era: You breathe fresh hope and promise, reminding me that the road is ever unfolding.

To my abundant family in Egypt, the roots of my being: The Hussein Salehs and the plethora of El-Ramlys—you are all amazing! Despite our distance and time, what is within you is within me.

To my forever friends, FIKJAMA: You've infused my days with laughter, light, and countless unforgettable moments. You've stood behind me (to support me), in front of me (to lead me), beside me (to love me), and sometimes behind me again (to let me lead). Love you, Farrah, Indra, Karen, Jeanette, Anita, and Anja, and your beautiful families.

To my modern-day friends, no acronyms, just deep love (in alphabetical order, because there's no order to love): Hannah along with Julie and Maysa; Jen & Alex with Aidan and Xander; Julia & David with Emilie; Kelly & David with Reid; Kristen with your crew; Lisa & Mike and your whole gang; Mitzi & Mark with Nico; Sheela and the curious Georges; Sherine with your girls; Tina and your crew; and Vickie & Steve and your incredible pack, including Brenda & Phil, Amy, Brent, and Grady. And, of course, all my fabulous neighbors of Trenton Place.

They say it takes a village, and our family has truly been blessed with an amazing one throughout the years from preschool to high school, at swimming pools and on soccer fields. My heartfelt appreciation goes especially to: Jennifer Brunetti, Mary Covington, Colleen Dupre, Mary Golden, Greg and Liz Jones, Kevin and Maret Jones, Leya Jones, Christian, Landon, and Lily Lauffer, Rob Norman, John Payne, Jeanne Pullen, Laura Sellers, Jan Schnurr, Della Smith, and Jen Stickleather.

To the family that we choose, or life chooses for us (depending on how long you've been in my life): Auntie Colleen; Lara & Henry and the boys; Safaa & Uncle Magdi with Hwaida, Adrian, Amir, and Amira & Donny; Sammy & Sonja, with the twins; Sandy & Omid; Sally; and Mariam & Osama with Ibo, Abdul, Karim, and Noor.

To the amazing Krishan: Thank you! Your genius support, delivered with incredible speed and ease, has been invaluable in amplifying inspirations, enhancing this book, and bringing the Mattain teachings more fully to life.

And to you, Mario: Without you, I wouldn't be where I am, expressing myself and sharing myself in so many mediums with the world. There are no words.

To my plethora of beta readers: The intuition you have provided me with and your willingness to support me have been so appreciated and invaluable. I see you, and I thank you. Special shout-outs to Anita, Deana, Farrah, Hannah, Ibo, Indra, Jeanne, Jen E, Jen T, Joe, Julie, Linus, Lisa, Millie, Mitzi, Safaa, Sherine, Tina, and Vickie—your feedback was crucial in shaping the words you read in the final version of this book!

To my book designer, Matt Davies: You are a pleasure to work with, and I'm excited to continue to create with you.

To Michael Ireland, my publisher: My heartfelt thanks to you for demystifying the publishing world. Your insight into the process provided essential understanding and was the catalyst for getting my children's book collection, THE SUPER YOU SERIES, underway.

To my amazing editor, Sage Taylor Kingsley: Thank you for the brilliant blend of editorial expertise, spiritual insight, and hilarious wit that elevated this book and made the process fun.

To all my incredible clients and followers: The daily outpouring of love from you constantly encourages me. Your courage to embrace change inspires me every day. Your engagement, feedback, and stories fill me with joy.

A heartfelt thank you to you, my amazing reader. I applaud you for being here. For your desire for truth. Here's to living life aligned with The Unconditional Three. Together, we're on this expedition of self-discovery and growth. Thank you for your trust and for being a part of this adventure. My appreciation for each and every one of you is boundless.

And finally, to God: Thank you for always being there for me. Especially when I can't feel it.

Life is amazing.

My Love, Always.
Manal

MATTAIN-SPEAK GLOSSARY

ACT—An acronym for Acceptance, Compassion, and Trust, this triad serves as as The Antidote to The Universal Fears. Not only does ACT stand as a direct counter-response to our intrinsic fears, but it also acts as a compass, guiding our alignment through life's complexities and challenges.

Acceptance—Rooted in the fear of failure, this term primarily addresses our physical experience. It speaks to self-acceptance, as well as the embracing of our life's journey and the greater mysteries of life. Acceptance ultimately guides us to an authentic sense of Worthiness.

Compassion—An emotional radiance that encompasses actions, feelings, thoughts, and beliefs directed towards ourselves, life, and the human journey. Compassion provides the bridge that helps us traverse feelings of not finding love, feeling unlovable, and unhappiness. It's the conduit to Love.

Trust—Our passage through life naturally elicits fears of the unknown, the uncontrollable, and ultimately, death. Cultivating Trust involves tapping into deeper meanings, placing faith in ourselves, our journey, and the vast mysteries and greater purpose of life. Trust is our bridge to innate, expansive Freedom.

ACTS—The embodiment of ACT, including Acceptance, Compassion, and Trust, culminates in Surrender, thus forming "ACTS." This progression signifies a route to a complete state of residing in our natural state of being.

Alignment—The harmonious natural state of our true selves—whether we refer to it as the soul, spirit, or inner light—shining radiantly. Achieved when The Four Bodies are flowing together and resistance free.

Antidote, The—For each of The Universal Fears there exists an antidote, which together combine to form a revolutionary framework. This trio of ACT—Acceptance, Compassion, and Trust—not only serves as a direct response to our innate fears, but also a compass for our alignment.

Anxiety—Expressions of unacknowledged fears regarding the future, anxiety is rooted deeply in The Four Bodies, influencing our self-perception, thoughts, feelings, and physical sensations. The Antidote lies in employing ACTS (Acceptance, Compassion, Trust, and Surrender) and embracing the power of presence.

Deconstructing the Key Lime Pie—The procedure of distinguishing the characteristics of our Four Bodies is like breaking down the layers of a Key Lime Pie. Just as this pie is layered with graham crackers, filling, whipped cream, and a cherry on top, identifying the expressions of The Four Bodies helps us fully grasp their unique characteristics. This process allows us to dissect these expressions and uncover our core truths.

Efforting—The act of exerting a disproportionate amount of Physical, Mental, Emotional, or Egoic energy towards a task or objective, resulting from and exacerbating a misalignment or resistance within one or more of The Four Bodies. Efforting thereby disrupts the natural state of flow, ease, and allowing; it often exhibits as a feeling of struggle or difficulty, detracting from seamless progression and fulfillment.

Four Bodies, The—An overarching Mattain concept referring to the Egoic, Emotional, Physical, and Mental aspects of an individual. Each Body has a distinct role when anxiety surfaces, illustrating the complex interplay among our varied dimensions.

    The Egoic Body—This Body holds our beliefs and self-perceptions. It's where we connect with specific labels and form our personal narratives.

The Mental Body—This Body comprises our thoughts, logic, and analysis. It also processes inputs from the other three Bodies.

The Emotional Body—This Body contains our feelings and serves as our emotional response center.

The Physical Body—This Body is where we sense the world around us, as well as inner indicators such as hunger, thirst, pain, and itchiness, through tangible sensations and symptoms.

Gap, The—That sacred, infinite space resting between inhalation and exhalation, offering a moment of pure presence and access to wholeness, stillness, and infinite truth.

Humaning—Engaging in the multifaceted and universal experiences inherent to being human, including the entirety of beliefs, thoughts, emotions, and actions that define our humanity. Humaning involves navigating through the complexities, joys, and unfolding of human existence, embracing and expressing the full spectrum of human emotions and situations while consciously participating in personal and collective evolution.

Mattain /mə'teɪ n/—A term crafted to symbolize the journey towards attaining your authentic life and living the existence you desire. The name "Mattain" is a derivative of "attain"—the English translation of "Manal"—and reflects the core purpose of The Mattain Method: to help you live your truest desires. While "attain" focuses on the achievement, "Mattain" emphasizes the process—the conduit to aligning with your authentic self.

Mattain Method, The—See Mattain Five-Step Process, Mattain Five Steps

Mattain Five-Step Process, Mattain Five Steps—This enlightening process process guides us to see, understand, and ultimately transform our fears into channels for recognizing our most profound desires. Steps 1-4 are active endeavors, while Step 5 symbolizes a state of mastery.

Step 1: Awareness—This step entails becoming conscious of our fears across all Four Bodies and recognizing that The Universal Fears exhibit as resistance within The Four Bodies. The fears reflect what is undesired.

Step 2: Acknowledgement—This process is the identification of our internal desires, directing us to The Unconditional Three. Once we're aware of what is undesired, which we uncovered in Step 1, we can easily identify what is desired.

Step 3: Appreciation—This practice involves valuing that our fears are guiding us towards our deeper desires. The potent antidote of ACT fosters genuine appreciation.

Step 4: Allowing—By moving through Steps 1-3, resistance has shifted from the undesired to a recognition of our desires; through Acceptance, Compassion, and Trust, we can begin to internally calibrate to a place of truth. Allowing naturally releases resistance.

Step 5: Surrender—Mastery of Steps 1 through 4 culminates in Step 5, where we find ourselves in a state of alignment with ACTS.

Muscling or Muscles—Just as building physical muscles like triceps at the gym requires consistent effort and dedication, building our "muscles" of alignment involves deliberate and continual practice. Embarking on the process of developing our alignment muscles, such as ACT and ACTS, enables us to fortify our inner truths and facilitate a stable foundation for personal growth and development. We engage in this undertaking mindfully and savor every step of enhancing our spiritual and emotional strength, resilience, and alignment.

PAINS—The common ways in which we resist our emotions is summed up in Mattain-Speak with "PAINS." These defensive mechanisms are common but unhelpful strategies. They can temporarily shield us from discomfort but also prevent us from healthily processing our emotions.

(P) Projecting involves deflecting our emotions onto others, diverting our attention away from self-reflection.

(A) Amplifying is the act of overstating or exaggerating our emotional reactions, which can create further emotional turmoil in the long run.

(I) Intellectualizing is when we explain away our feelings, focusing on understanding them logically rather than experiencing them. "First-world problems" and "I should be thankful" are two common statements that intellectualize our experience.

(N) Negating involves invalidating or denying our emotions, telling ourselves that we shouldn't feel a certain way, thereby avoiding our true emotional state.

(S) Suppressing is the conscious or unconscious act of avoiding or burying our emotions, a tactic that might provide temporary relief but could lead to significant emotional or physical health problems if these emotions are not eventually addressed.

PAINS-ing/ed—Engaging or having engaged in PAINS.

Resistance—Resistance refers to any form of obstruction or barrier within The Four Bodies—Physical, Emotional, Mental, and Egoic—that impedes our pursuit of alignment. It appears differently within each Body, acting as a hindrance that keeps us from fully engaging with our authentic truth.

Seeing—Synonymous with Awareness. With seeing comes liberty.

Surrender—This term represents the apex of alignment across The Four Bodies, signifying a state of unconditional Acceptance, Compassion, and Trust, abbreviated as ACT, towards all that exists. Surrender is an active embrace of life in its entirety. It encompasses mastery over life, expertise in applying The Mattain Five-Step Process, and an acknowledgement that every life experience brings its own gift.

Unconditional Three, The—These represent Worthiness, Love, and Freedom, which are inborn navigators guiding us towards fulfillment and self-realization. Every manifestation of anxiety or fear acts not as an obstacle, but a mirror, reflecting opportunities to recalibrate and realign with these fundamental aspects of our being. This approach does not merely address fear but leverages it, channeling its energy to propel us towards our desires for Worthiness, Love, and Freedom.

Universal Fears, The—The three universal fears within the Egoic Body:

> **Fear of Inadequacy and/or Unworthiness**—Our Egoic Body is where we form perceptions of worthiness. Here, we constantly evaluate ourselves, our actions, and our worth based on the standards set by society and ourselves. We tend to compare our lives with those of others, and these comparisons lead to feelings of inadequacy and unacknowledged fears about our worthiness. Remember, everyone's life is unique and cannot be compared. Yet the Egoic Body sometimes overlooks this sentiment, leading to a materialization of anxiety.

> **Fear of Never Achieving Love or Lasting Happiness**—The constant pursuit of happiness, love, peace, joy, or as some may call it, the "ultimate state of being." Yet the road taken to achieve this state is riddled with unacknowledged fears. The struggle to achieve these states can feel like an endless chase. The more we seek them, the more elusive they can become.

Fear of Loss of Freedom, Death, Uncertainty or Loss of Control—One of the fundamental struggles we face in our Egoic Body is the fear of the unknown and accompanying loss of control. We inhabit an unpredictable world where we cannot control life or death. As a result, our ego yearns for predictability and seeks to exert control as a means of feeling secure. The essential nature of this human journey—the "game of life"—is its unmistakable uncertainty about what tomorrow holds.

Note: Certain unique Mattain concepts are capitalized to underscore their significance within the framework. However, specific descriptors or components of these overarching terms are presented in lowercase to maintain fluidity and ease of reading.

ABOUT THE AUTHOR

Life is a dance of growth, understanding, and alignment. I am privileged to share the steps I've learned along the way, hoping they guide you to dancing to your own beat.

With the intellect of an engineer and soul of a spiritual guide, Manal is a lifelong seeker who masterfully blends metaphysical insights with the precision of an analytical mind. This unique combination, fortified by over thirty years of professional, entrepreneurial, and personal experience, has allowed her to deconstruct complex human behavior into its essential elements and develop a simple roadmap for navigating the road to self-alignment. Her Five-Step, Four-Body Framework, which leverages inquisitive rigor and deep compassion, has been honed through years of personal and interpersonal practice. Her unparalleled system empowers others to reclaim their intrinsic Worthiness, Love, and Freedom.

Manal brings a rare blend of authenticity, humor, and wisdom to the art of self-discovery. In her celebrated TEDx Talk, "Why You Don't Need to Search for Your Purpose," she challenges conventional notions about purpose and helps listeners connect with their wholeness. She is featured as an Insight Time teacher and in Om Yoga Magazine. Her live sessions, renowned for their experiential depth, playful exploration of resistance, and genuine connection, have helped thousands to release limiting beliefs, embrace vulnerability, and connect with their true selves. She is known for her ability to make complex spiritual concepts easy and has an innate ability to lead others to surrender to the flow of life.

Manal lives in North Carolina with her family and beloved twin cats. She enjoys yoga, meditation, and long walks in Umstead State Park. She has a particular fondness for sushi and loves her coffee! She's also an avid traveler, and especially enjoys visits to family in Vancouver, British Columbia; Los Angeles, California; and Cairo, Egypt.

BOOK CLUB & SELF-DISCOVERY QUESTIONS

Enjoy the following questions to deepen your reflection and application of *Transcending Anxiety: From Fear to Freedom.*

Personal Resonance:

- Which chapter or concept resonated most deeply with your personal experiences? Why?

- Were there moments in the book where you felt a strong connection to or disconnection from the author's perspective?

Applying Insights:

- Based on the strategies presented, what are the next steps you plan to take in your journey of moving beyond anxiety and fear?

- Which techniques are you most inclined to incorporate into your daily life?

Challenging Beliefs:

- Were there sections in the book that challenged your existing beliefs about anxiety and fear?

- How has your perspective changed?

The Author's Lens:

- How do you think Manal's personal experiences influenced the strategies and insights in the book?

- If you could ask Manal one question, what would it be? Feel free to reach out at **www.mattain.com/connect**!

Comparing and Contrasting:

- If you've used other resources on anxiety and fear, how does this book's approach stand out?

- Compared to other resources, how is Manal's voice/style different?

- Has this book made you feel something you haven't felt from other content?

Sharing and Forwarding:

- How would you describe the core message of this book to a friend? Is there a particular quote or short section you feel compelled to share with others? (I give you my unconditional approval to do so!)

Looking Ahead:

- How do you envision revisiting this book in the future? Will you use it as a reference, guide, or source of comfort?

- Based on your reading, what would you like to explore further?

Final Note:

Let's turn "Mattain Moment" into "Mattain Movement!" Join our tribe at **www.mattain.com/community** to share your insights, connect with others, and continue your work of overcoming anxiety and unraveling the myriads of life's mysteries and wonders.

For Book Clubs:

If you're seeking a list of further questions for in-depth book club discussions, please visit **www.mattain.com/bookclub.**

Put the 5-4-3-2-1 into action!

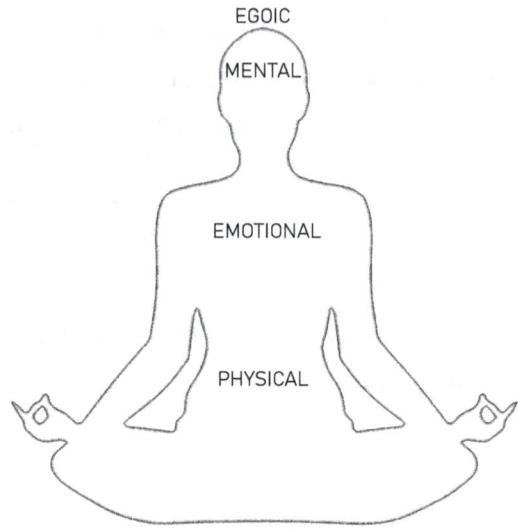

Dear Reader,

The final page of Transcending Anxiety marks a beginning—the start of putting The Mattain Method into practice for the rest of your life.

5 Steps, 4 Bodies, 3 Desires, 2 States, and 1 Truth. They're not just concepts to understand, but principles to live by. It's time to move from knowing to feeling your way to liberation, from resistance to surrender, from anxiety to your authentic power. I invite you to continue this exploration with me, applying these tools every day. Let's question, explore, and feel our way to Worthiness, Love, and Freedom.

Here is a Bonus Gift for you!

A Transcending Anxiety Meditation Series, featuring:

- Four-Body Scan: Reconnect and Align with Your Inner Power

- Emotional Body Scan: A Practice for Presence and Peace

- Transcending Anxiety: Identify and Release Your Fears

- Mattain Five-Step Meditation: Your Daily Practice for Lasting Freedom

- Embodying Presence: A Four Bodies Meditation

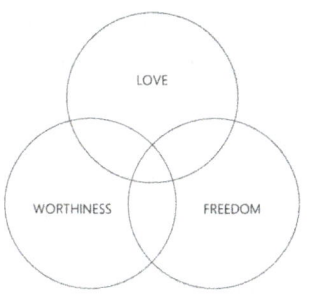

Exclusive Bonus! Get the Practices for Alignment Guide—your personalized roadmap for strengthening each of your Four Bodies—completely FREE. Discover simple yet powerful practices to nurture lasting wholeness.

Audio Mattain Moments: Listen anytime! Guided recordings of every Mattain Moment exercise from this book, led personally.

Stop thinking your way to freedom; start feeling it. Go to **www.mattain.com/justforyou** to continue your path to Worthiness, Love, and Freedom.

Your path is uniquely yours, but you don't need to walk it alone. Join our Mattain Tribe! We're all about sharing, supporting, and cheering each other on as we navigate this beautiful human experience.

Follow my ongoing adventures, reflections, and discoveries:

- Facebook: Mattain by Manal
- Instagram: @mattainbymanal
- LinkedIn: Manal El-Ramly

- TikTok: @mattainbymanal
- YouTube: Mattain by Manal
- Goodreads: Manal El-Ramly
- Go to **www.mattain.com/justforyou** to get started.

Thank you for sharing this amazing life with me.

MATTAIN MOMENTS

www.ingramcontent.com/pod-product-compliance
Lightning Source LLC
Chambersburg PA
CBHW070547130626
46556CB00001B/53